INVENTORY 1985

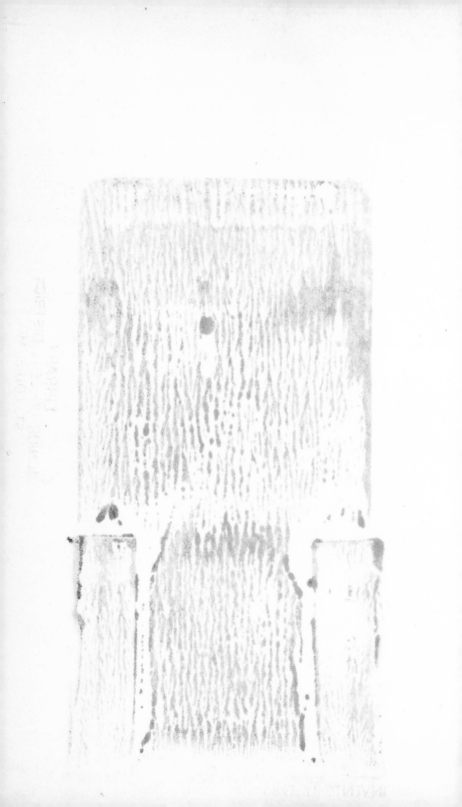

The English Civil War and after, 1642-1658

The English Civil War and after, 1642-1658

EDITED BY
R. H. PARRY

Contributors
Robert Ashton, Brian Manning, D. H. Pennington,
Ivan Roots, C. V. Wedgwood, Austin Woolrych

UNIVERSITY OF CALIFORNIA PRESS
Berkeley and Los Angeles   1970

First published by
MACMILLAN AND CO LTD

Printed in Great Britain

University of California Press
Berkeley and Los Angeles

Library of Congress Catalog Card Number: 74-111423
SBN: 520 01695 5

Contents

Preface   vii

List of Abbreviations   viii

1 The Outbreak of the English Civil War   1
   BRIAN MANNING

2 The Rebels of 1642   22
   D. H. PENNINGTON

3 The Trial of Charles I   41
   C. V. WEDGWOOD

4 Oliver Cromwell and the Rule of the Saints   59
   AUSTIN WOOLRYCH

5 Swordsmen and Decimators – Cromwell's Major-Generals   78
   IVAN ROOTS

6 The Civil War and the Class Struggle   93
   ROBERT ASHTON

7 Interest – Public, Private and Communal   111
   IVAN ROOTS

   Notes on Contributors   122

   Index   125

Preface

For several years past it has been the custom at Eton College to give a course of revision lectures to history specialists about to take their 'A' levels. These have normally concerned the Special Subject paper and have been delivered by members of the History department. Partly as a change, but mainly in the belief that the study of history in Sixth Forms now more closely approximates to the work of university undergraduates in the subject, it was decided to invite some of the most prominent scholars of the Great Rebellion of the seventeenth century to come to Eton to deliver lectures on topics of their own selection. All but one of the essays had their origin in this decision and the exception is the second essay by Professor Roots, which was written specially for this book.

No one who has taught history for any length of time to Sixth Forms can fail to realise that his main problem is to keep up to date with current research and current publications. This degree of specialisation may have some disadvantages but it is nevertheless a fact. It is hoped therefore, that this volume will elucidate some aspects of the seventeenth century which now interest all students of the period.

Practically no alteration has been made to the manuscripts submitted by the authors and the function of the editor has been administrative rather than scholarly. In most cases full references have been included for those who care to use them, but this is not so with Dame Veronica Wedgwood's 'The Trial of Charles I' because her lecture was a specially condensed version of her excellent and popular book on the subject.

R. H. Parry

Eton
May 1969

List of Abbreviations

BM	British Museum
Cal. S. P. Dom.	*Calendar of State Papers Domestic*
CJ	[*House of*] *Commons' Journals*
Econ. Hist. Rev.	*Economic History Review*
EHR	*English Historical Review*
HJ	*Historical Journal*
HMC	Historical Manuscripts Commission
JBS	*Journal of British Studies*
JMH	*Journal of Modern History*
LJ	[*House of*] *Lords' Journals*
PP	*Past and Present*
PRO	Public Record Office, London
SP	State Papers, Public Record Office
TRHS	*Transactions of the Royal Historical Society*
TSP	*The State Papers of John Thurloe* (ed. T. Birch, 1742)

1. The Outbreak of the English Civil War

BRIAN MANNING

THE members of the Long Parliament were for the most part well-to-do landowners, nobility and gentry, who shared similar social and educational backgrounds, similar economic interests, and similar ideas on religion and politics. They disliked 'popery' and what they regarded as the 'popish' tendencies of Archbishop Laud and his party, who had dominated the church during the 1630s. But they were not inclined towards presbyterianism and they feared the more radical puritans and 'sectaries'. Although they had no love for bishops, most of them wished to keep episcopal government of the church, provided that it could be reformed so as to be under the supervision of the common law and parliament and the squirearchy; and provided that the bishops were men of the same middle-of-the-road views in religion as most of the nobility and gentry. They disliked the policies and methods of government of Charles I in the 1630s; but once unpopular taxes such as Ship-money had been made illegal, unpopular courts like Star Chamber and High Commission abolished, and the summoning of a parliament at least once in every three years assured by the Triennial Act, there remained only one obstacle to agreement between the king and the two Houses of Parliament – distrust.

Could Charles I be trusted to act moderately and keep within the limits imposed on him by the legislation of the Long Parliament? A majority of the House of Commons and a minority of the House of Lords answered in the negative: the king was still surrounded by evil advisers and he could not be trusted until the Privy Council and government offices were filled by men in whom 'parliament may have cause to confide'. A majority of the House of Lords and a minority of the House of Commons answered in the affirmative: the time had come to give the king the benefit of the doubt and not antagonise him further by restricting his right to choose his own counsellors and officers. Charles asked whether there would be any end to the demands of the majority in the House of Commons: so far he had agreed to all they asked but without being able to win their confidence, and still they made more demands.

He distrusted the leaders of the House of Commons and their friends in
the House of Lords, and suspected them of ambition for power and of
a secret design to convert the monarchy into a virtual republic. He
refused to surrender his right to choose his own advisers. He could count
on the support of a majority of the House of Lords, and he might have
been able to gain the support of a majority in the House of Commons if
at this moment he had not embarked upon a course of action which
intensified distrust of his intentions.

Charles was persuaded that the discontent of the majority of the
Commons was due to the machinations of a small faction. He believed
that if the trouble-makers were removed or discredited the loyalty to
the crown and instinctive conservatism of the majority would reassert
itself. So he accused six of the leaders, one peer and five members of the
House of Commons, of treason, and on 4 January 1642 went in person to
the House of Commons with armed guards in an unsuccessful attempt
to arrest the five members. 'The attempt on the Five Members' confirmed the majority's distrust of the king and their confidence in their
leaders. It also disquieted those members of the two Houses who were
coming to prefer the risks of trusting the king to the dangers of continuing disagreement between the king and the House of Commons and
between the House of Commons and the House of Lords. But although
such men had their confidence in the king shaken and were reluctant to
take his side, they shared his distrust of the leaders of the House of
Commons.

In the early part of 1642 only two small minorities saw a resort to
force as either necessary or inevitable. There were a few wholehearted
royalists who for some time had been telling the king that if he did not
show a willingness to defend his rights by force he would never be able
to stop the steady erosion of his power; and there were a few radical
puritans who were ready to resort to force to bring about sweeping
changes in the government and doctrine of the church. But the vast
majority of the two Houses of Parliament, of the nobility and gentry in
general, of the government officers, of the lawyers, of the mayors and
aldermen of towns, of the leading merchants, in other words, the
great bulk of the governing classes, still deplored the thought of resol-
ving the disagreement by force, and still hoped for and expected agreement between king, Lords and Commons. Yet they were steadily
being divided into two parties during 1642; parliamentarians, who
distrusted the king and demanded more restrictions on his power, at
least for a time until they could trust him with greater power again; and

royalists, who were unhappy about reducing the power of the crown too much, and longed to be able to trust the king. This was not a division over religious or political ends. Thus men from the same social background and with the same economic interests, with similar political and religious ideas, found themselves in opposite parties, for the decision they had to take in 1642 was not a decision about the best form of government for the church or for the state, nor about changes in the social or the economic order, but simply whether or not to trust Charles I. Men of the same class and the same political and religious views gave different answers to this question and found themselves on opposite sides; men of different classes and different political and religious views gave the same answer to this question and found themselves on the same side. Many of those who distrusted the king and regarded his obstinacy as the only obstacle to agreement consented to the raising of an army under the command of the Earl of Essex because they thought that a show of force would make the king more reasonable. They believed that no more than a show of force would be necessary because the king appeared to have few supporters and small means to raise an army: he would not be able to fight and would be obliged to negotiate. But the king proved to have more supporters and greater resources than at first appeared. For many were willing to trust him now that he seemed almost powerless. They did not wish to see him forced into an abject surrender which would permanently weaken the crown. They supported him because they thought that when parliament saw that he had the means to fight it would moderate its demands and reach an agreement without bloodshed. So by the end of the summer of 1642 there were two armies on foot in England, and the country found that it had drifted into a civil war that few wanted to fight.

Distrust was the main obstacle to agreement between king and parliament, but it might not have been an insurmountable obstacle without the conjuncture of other factors, which involved the lower classes in the crisis and drove a deeper wedge into the ruling class. These other factors were the fear of papists, the sharp decline of trade and industry, and an upsurge of class-feeling and class-hostility.

On 5 May 1641 the crisis over the Earl of Strafford was approaching a climax. The Bill of Attainder had passed the Commons and was now before the Lords. The king was making desperate efforts to save the earl from execution: it was still doubtful whether the bill would pass the Lords, and, if it did, even more doubtful whether the king could be brought to give his consent. Parliament and London were beset with fears. It was known that there had been a plot to rescue Strafford from the Tower; it was believed that there was a design to bring the army to London to overawe the parliament; and it was rumoured that a French army was coming to the aid of the royal family.[1] A debate in the House of Commons was interrupted by a sudden noise from the direction of the gallery:

> The gentlemen in the gallery most of them ran away into the committee chamber, where they drew their swords. . . . All the gentlemen under the gallery in an amaze leaped down, and some fell one upon another; some ran away out of the House, as my Lord Cranborne, and others. The people also running amazed through Westminster Hall, old Sir Robert Mansell drew his sword, and bade them stand like true Englishmen, no man being able to report the cause of their fright; but no man stayed with him. But he advanced alone out of the Hall towards the House of Commons, with his sword drawn. Mr Thomas Earle broke his shin, and Sir Frederick Cornwallis had his hat all dusted with lime . . .[2]

The cry spread through London 'that the Papists had set the Lower House on fire, and had beset it with arms'. 'In a clap all the city is in alarum; shops closed; a world of people in arms runs down to Westminster.'[3] When they got there the panic was over and its cause had been discovered – a fat member had dropped a paper over the back of the gallery and in bending down to pick it up 'with his weight broke a few lathes, which made a sudden noise'.[4]

Fear of papists reached panic proportions in the autumn of 1641 when the Catholics in Ireland rose in rebellion and slaughtered the Protestants. Richard Baxter wrote that 'there was nothing that with the people wrought so much, as the Irish Massacre and Rebellion. . . . This filled all England with a fear both of the Irish, and of the papists at home. . . . Insomuch, that when the rumour of a plot was occasioned at London, the poor people, all the counties over, were ready either to run to arms, or hide themselves, thinking that the papists were ready to rise and cut their throats.'[5]

On 12 November 1641 Sir William Acton, an alderman of London, brought to the House of Commons John Davis, servant of an inn at Ross in Herefordshire, who had come to London and told an alarming story to the alderman's coachman. Davis was 'a plain country-fellow, and not able so fully to express himself', but his story was that he had acted as a guide to several gentlemen who had come to his inn and wanted to get to Raglan Castle, the seat of the Earl of Worcester, a Catholic. There a groom took Davis's horse to a stable where there were about sixty horses. Then the groom showed him a vault underground where he told him there were another forty horses, and another place underground where furniture for about 100 or 120 horses was kept, 'with great store of match and powder, and other ammunition belonging to war', enough 'for about 2000 men'. 'He told me', continued Davis, 'that his master the Earl of Worcester, gave notice privately, that any man would be entertained, should have thirteen pence a day, good pay from him, in case they would be true to him. . . . He told me that his master had at this time 700 men under pay.' Davis's story was published in a pamphlet, which concluded with the query: 'Whether we have not as just cause to fear the Papists in England, as they had in Ireland and Wales, and if they should once take a head, and be not prevented, what evil consequence may ensue thereof?'[6]

Then on 15 November a young man named Thomas Beale came to the door of the House of Commons 'and sent in word that he had matters of a high nature to reveal'. He was a tailor and was probably out of work and in some sort of trouble with the law. Being without lodgings he had decided to spend the night in a ditch on Moor Fields, an open space to the north of the city where the citizens went for recreation. There, so he told the House of Commons, he overheard two gentlemen talking about a plot. 'There was 108 men appointed to kill 108 persons of the Parliament, every one his man; some were lords, and the others were to be members of the House of Commons, all puritans . . .'; '. . . those that were to kill the lords were brave gallants, in their scarlet-coats, and had received every man £10 a-piece . . .'; those that were to kill the members of the House of Commons had 40s each, and 'Dick Jones was appointed to kill that rascally puritan Pym; and that four tradesmen, citizens, were to kill the puritan citizens which were parliament-men'. The assassinations were to take place on the night of 18 November, as the members were 'coming down stairs, or taking their coaches, or entering into their lodgings, or any other way as they should see opportunity'; and while London was in tumult, the papists would rise in Warwickshire, Worcestershire, Buckinghamshire, Lancashire, and two 'other places he remembers not'. The object was to prevent the sending of forces from England against the Catholics in Ireland, 'because, if they prevailed there, they should not have cause to fear here'.[7]

Sir Robert Harley, a member of the House of Commons, after hearing these stories, wrote to his wife at Brampton Bryan in Herefordshire, warning her of the danger of a rising of the papists and instructing her to put the house in a state of defence. He also wrote to John Aston at Ludlow to 'look well to your town, for the papists are discovered to have a bloody design, in general, as well against this kingdom as elsewhere'. On the night of 19 November rumours spread through Herefordshire, Worcester and Shropshire that the papists had risen. '. . . At Brampton Bryan they were all in arms upon the top of Sir Robert's castle, and took up provisions thither with them, and in great fear. . . .' It would seem that the panic spread from Brampton Bryan, which is in the northern-most parts of Herefordshire on the border with Shropshire, along the main road to the east as far as Kidderminster, on the way gripping Ludlow and then Bewdley, where it 'caused them all in the town to be up in arms, with watch all night in very great fear'. And so to Kidder-minster; then it sped north to Bridgnorth, where the bailiffs and towns-men made a great fire in the high street, near the market cross, and kept watch all night, fortifying their courage with beer and mulled sack. In one night a rumour had been carried fifty-five miles. The next day, the fact that this rumour proved to be false did little to reassure Lady Harley, who reported to her husband:

> I have, according to your directions caused a good provision of bullets to be made and the pieces charged. There are no men in the house except Samuel and another. I do not propose this out of fear, but out of care for the children, whether you think it would be best for me and the children with no more servants than necessary to take a house in some town. I think Shrewsbury is the best to go to. If the Papists should rise or there should be any commotion, to my apprehension a town is safest. . . . If we should be put to it, I do not believe we at Brampton should be able to stand siege. . . .[8]

The king failed in his attempt to arrest the Five Members on 4 January 1642, but he had gathered some hundreds of armed men, many of them ex-soldiers of the army that he had raised to fight the Scots in 1640, and the Five Members were known to be in London. The city was tense and fearful. Nehemiah Wallington, a turner who lived in Little Eastcheap, recorded the fears that filled the minds of the citizens during these days: the king 'hath armies of men come out of the north parts, with fierce countenances, and with deadly weapons, that puts all us citizens in great fear that there is no good meant towards us'; the papists have made lists of those lords, members of parliament, ministers, and citizens that they will kill; 'and I heard of deadly weapons newly made, which were to be struck into the body, and could not be pulled out again'. To the mind of a puritan like Wallington all this seemed all the more likely because the sins of the citizens had provoked God to hand them over to their enemies for destruction. On Twelfth Night, 6 January 1642, the alarm was raised 'that the king and cavaliers, with fifteen hundred horse, were coming to surprise the city' and fetch in the Five Members by force. Wallington never forgot the terror of that night. '. . . We heard (as we lay in our beds) a great cry in the streets that there were horse and foot coming against the city', and there was a tremendous banging on his door and shouts of 'Arm, Arm'. '. . . Fear and trembling entered on all'; 'some women being with child were so affrighted therewith as they miscarried', and the wife of an alderman (a neighbour of Wallington) died of fright. Within an hour thousands of men were in the streets in their full arms, and many thousands more with halberds, swords, clubs and such weapons as they could lay their hands on. The gates of the city were shut, the portcullises lowered, and the chains put across the streets to stop horses. Women brought stools, forms and tubs from their houses to build barricades, and boiled water 'to throw on the cavaliers'. But when the Lord Mayor ascertained that there were no forces coming against the city and reassured the citizens that they were safe, the streets emptied as fast as they had filled 'and every man retired to his house'. The cause of the alarm was variously reported to have been the accidental discharge of a carbine in Covent Garden, where many of the king's guard of ex-soldiers had their lodgings, or some men from a troop of horse, which had been raised for service in Ireland and billeted at Barnet, riding near London and being taken for 'the fore-runners of 500 horse that were that night to come into the City'.[9] In the minds of men and women living in fear of being murdered in their beds, 'papists' and 'evil advisers' and 'cavaliers' and 'delinquents' were rolled into a single malevolent being, lying hidden everywhere, in cities and in country houses, and poised for attack, to kill, plunder, burn and destroy all honest and decent people.

If the king had contemplated making an attempt to fetch the Five Members out of the City, he abandoned it in face of the mood of London and fled from his capital on 10 January, the day before the Five Members were carried back to Westminster in triumph by the citizens. On 7 January the news had reached Buckinghamshire that their member John Hampden was one of the five charged with treason by the king. A crowd of several thousand assembled and resolved to march on London to defend their member. The news of their approach disturbed some members of parliament, who urged that they be turned back, but the majority decided to take no action and the Buckinghamshire men arrived on 11 January, the day the Five Members returned to Westminster: 'There was above three thousand on horseback, every man with his protestation in his hand, intimating that they had petition to present to the Honourable Court; the others were on foot; but they reached in all from the Exchange to Newgate, three and four in a rank, coming to Westminster. . . .'[10] During January and February 1642, almost every day, columns of men on horse and on foot swung through London on their way to Westminster to deliver petitions to the two Houses. On 20 January 6000 came from Essex, and on 25 January three or four thousand from Hertfordshire.[11] On 8 February petitioners marched in from Kent: 'These Kentish men I did see myself come up Fish Street Hill', wrote Nehemiah Wallington, 'many hundred of them, on horseback, with their protestations sticking in their hats and girdles; they came in order, three in a rank, first the knights, and gentlemen, then about twenty ministers, then the other horse and footmen.'[12] On 10 February a petition was brought in from Northamptonshire, 'the best attended by gentlemen of quality of any petition that hath been yet delivered'.[13] 'Near a thousand' people arrived in London on 15 February with a petition from Leicestershire, and two days later between fifteen hundred and three thousand from Sussex, led by their sheriff, followed by knights, gentlemen and freeholders, 'on horseback, ranked in a decent manner'.[14] These were well-organised demonstrations fully under the control of the gentry leaders of the county communities, and faithfully reflecting a well-ordered social hierarchy. But the House of Commons became uneasy when it heard that sixteen or seventeen thousand people had assembled in the cloth-manufacturing districts of Suffolk and Essex and were planning to march on London. In obedience to the orders of parliament the greater part of the crowd dispersed after signing a petition, leaving just 1000 to carry it to London on 9 February.[15]

The object of all these petitions was to put pressure on the House of Lords to consent to the demands of the majority of the House of Commons for the removal of evil counsellors from about the king, for the expulsion of bishops and popish peers from the House of Lords, and for the putting the Tower of London, the forts and militia of the kingdom into the hands of such persons as the two Houses could trust. Fears of foreign invasion and of insurrection by the papists were constantly expressed, and the disarming and confining of all papists repeatedly demanded. But the most prominent theme in all these petitions was the decay of trade and industry. The mayor, aldermen and other inhabitants of Colchester complained to the House of Commons: '. . . We find the trade of clothing, and new drapery, upon which the livelihoods of many thousands, men, women and children in this town do depend, to be almost wholly decayed, and poverty abundantly to grow upon us.' The people of Essex told the two Houses: 'Our trading, especially of clothing and farming', which are 'the two trades of our county, whereby the multitudes of our people have lived', 'grow apace to so great a damp, as many thousands are like to come to sudden want', and 'we tremble to think, what may follow thereupon.'[16] The clothiers of Suffolk and Essex petitioned the king as well as the two Houses of Parliament that the merchants of London have ceased to buy cloth for export and 'our cloths for the most part, for the space of this eighteen months remain upon our hands, our stocks lying dead therein, and we can maintain our trading no longer: the cries for food of many thousands of poor, who depend on this trade, do continually press us, not without threats, and some beginnings of mutinies: so that, if some speedy relief do not intervene, we can expect no less than confusion.'[17] The people of Suffolk warned the House of Lords 'of the stop of trade, especially that of clothing, upon which the estates and livelihoods of many thousands do depend, who very lately, in regard of their wants, by their speeches and gestures, express sad intentions of disturbing our public peace if they be not speedily prevented'.[18] The mayor, aldermen and common council of Exeter informed the Lords of petitions from citizens 'wherein they present the great decay and deadness in the trades of the said city, especially in the manufactures of serges or perpetuanyet', and declared 'that (unless God by some speedy and timely remedy do prevent it) this city and county are like greatly to be endangered, by reason of the decay of commerce (with its inseparable companion poverty), which will, as they justly fear, stir up many thousand persons to insolent and outrageous actions'.[19] These complaints were repeated by Gloucester and Marlborough, and by the clothiers of another great centre of cloth manufacture, the West Riding of Yorkshire.[20] Hertfordshire spoke of 'the total decay of trade, and great scarcity of money, and thereby the impoverishing and unsettlement of the whole kingdom . . .'; and Northamptonshire begged the House of Lords 'to take into consideration the distressed state of the poorer sort of people, who, for want of trade and employment, are brought to extremity, which (without timely prevention) may prove of dangerous consequence'.[21]

The paralysis of the economy had spread outwards from London, where the merchants had ceased to trade owing to the fears and uncertainties of the political situation. This the petitions blamed on the continuing disagreements between king, Lords and Commons, which they attributed to the influence of the king's evil advisers and of the presence of a popish party in the House of Lords. 'Amid these events the trade of this city and kingdom is stopping altogether', reported the Venetian ambassador. 'The ordinary course of all trade has been interrupted and those who obtain their daily food by the work of their hands alone are reduced to the limits of despair. These ignorant people' are 'persuaded . . . that these calamities proceed from the presence of the bishops and Catholic lords in Parliament . . .'[22] The lord mayor, aldermen and commuo council of the City of London petitioned the House of Lords on 25 January that

> . . . they cannot but represent further to your lordships, that very
> many thousands of clothiers and handicraftsmen and their families,
> who have their dependence for their livelihood upon this city, do
> daily more and more make sad moans and lamentable cries that they
> are no way able any longer to subsist, because the petitioners and others
> do not buy off their wares as formerly they did; that the petitioners
> cannot so do till trade be quickened by the speedy relief of Ireland,
> till Papists be fully disarmed, and the strength of the kingdom by
> land and sea put into the hands of such as the Parliament may
> confide in, through want whereof the trade of the kingdom is fallen
> to so low an ebb, that the petitioners are not able longer to proceed
> therein as formerly; which necessitated forbearance of trade and
> scarcity of money, will (as they verily believe) in very short time cast
> innumerable multitudes of those poor men into such a depth of
> poverty and extremity, as will enforce them upon some dangerous and
> desperate attempts not fit to be expressed, much less justified. . . .[23]

By 40 votes to 32 the House of Lords refused to join with the Commons in a petition to the king to put the Tower, forts and militia of the kingdom 'into the hands of such persons as your Parliament may confide in, and as shall be recommended unto your Majesty by both Houses of Parliament'. The minority protested that this was 'absolutely necessary to the settling of the present distempers' and 'to the furtherance of trade, now much obstructed and decayed'.[24] At a conference Pym warned the Lords of the danger of tumults and insurrections of the meaner sort of people, by reason of their ill vent of cloth and other manufactures, whereby great multitudes are set on work, who live for the most part on their daily gettings, and will in a very short time be brought to great extremity, if not employed; nothing is more sharp and pressing than necessity and want; what they cannot buy, they will take; and from them the like necessity will quickly be derived to the farmers and husbandmen, and so grow higher, and involve all in an equality of misery and distress, if it be not prevented. . . .[25]

On 26 January apprentices and seamen of London petitioned the Lords that 'trading is extraordinarily decayed, and fears greatly multiplied . . . by reason of the exposedness of this kingdom unto dangers foreign and intestine'; they demanded the names of those who were obstructing the putting of the kingdom into a position to be able to defend itself, and the removal of 'the heavy pressures lying upon us, and growing insupportable by the delay of relief': 'your petitioners greatly fearing, that, if present remedy be not afforded, from the hands of this honourable Parliament (as from wise physicians), multitudes will be ready to take hold upon that remedy which is next at hand; "Oppression" (as Solomon saith) "maketh wise men mad" '.[26] On 31 January hundreds of artificers and poor people gathered in Moor Fields and marched to the House of Commons with a petition protesting that they were 'utterly impoverished' by the great decay of trade which was caused by the prevalency of the bishops, papists and a malignant faction in the House of Lords. They said they had spent all their money and could not get bread to eat, 'so that unless some speedy remedy be taken for the removal of all such obstructions, which hinders the happy progress of your great endeavours, your petitioners shall not rest in quietness, but shall be enforced to lay hold on the next remedy which is at hand, to remove the disturbers of our peace; want and necessity breaking the bounds of modesty, and rather than your petitioners will suffer themselves and their families to perish through hunger and misery, (though hitherto patiently groaned under) they cannot leave any means unessayed for their relief'. They demanded that the obstructors of the proceedings of the parliament may be named, 'and that noble worthies of the House of Peers, who concur with you in your happy votes, may be earnestly desired to join with this Honourable House, and to sit and vote as one entire body, which we hope will remove from us our distracted fears, and prevent that which oppression will make the wisest and peaceablest

men to put in execution'.[27] The House of Commons sent Denzil
Hollis to inform the Lords of this petition. 'He said, there were some
things in the petition extraordinary, which at another time the parliament should be tender of; but now, considering the necessity of a
multitude, the House of Commons thinks it not good to waken a sleepy
lion; for it would pull on the mischief sooner.' '. . . They have not bread
to put in their mouths', Hollis told the Lords: 'relief they must have,
which must be by setting them to work: that cannot be but by settling
of trade, and restoring it: trade will not be settled till these fears and
distractions be taken away: fears will not remove till we see a change,
that the great affairs of our kingdom be carried in another channel;
that those evil counsellors be removed who have discomposed our
frame of this commonwealth; that we may secure ourselves, and be in
a posture of defence; whereas we are now exposed to dangers, and no
man is sure of anything but what he carries about him: till this be, we
cannot expect trade should run in such a way as that the poor may be
set on work.'[28] On 1 February the Houses were besieged by hundreds of
women crying for bread,[29] and the next day a petition was delivered to
the Commons in the name of 15,000 'poor labouring men, known by the
name of porters, and the lowest members of the city'. They said that
they were without employment and having sold or pawned what little
they possessed, they were unable to pay the rents for their lodgings and
were 'very nigh turning into the streets'. Soon they would be forced
'to extremities, not fit to be named, and to make good that saying,
"That necessity hath no law"; it is true, that we have nothing to lose but
our lives'.[30] Under this pressure the conservative majority in the House
of Lords collapsed on 1 and 2 February and the peers joined with the
Commons in a petition to the king 'to put the Tower of London, and all
other forts, and the whole militia of the kingdom, into the hands of
such persons as shall be recommended unto your Majesty by both
Houses of Parliament . . .'.[31] From this moment the parliamentarians
dominated both Houses.

   In dealing with this crucial question of the control of the forts and
the militia, the minds of members of both Houses were directed to the
economic crisis, with its attendant risks of popular disorders, rather
than to the constitutional and political issues involved in the actual
demand made by the two Houses. It was the apparent worsening of the
economic crisis that provided the growing pressure for agreement
between the two Houses, for the crisis was thought to have been caused
by their disagreements. So they agreed to the demand in relation to

the forts and the militia because it was represented as the only way to
end the fears of merchants and revive the confidence necessary for
trade and industry to grow again. In the eyes of moderate members of
both Houses the need for co-operation between king and parliament
was made more urgent by an economic crisis which dwarfed all other
considerations; and they joined in the demand for the king to end the
deadlock by giving way to a political and constitutional measure which
they would not have seen as necessary or desirable on political and
constitutional grounds, but which they now saw as the only alternative
to economic collapse and popular tumults. But the king would not give
way and the political deadlock became more complete.

'Papists', 'evil advisers', 'cavaliers' and 'a malignant faction' of the
nobility and gentry were represented as holding the king a virtual
captive and preventing him from making the necessary concessions to
end the political deadlock and revive trading. So the civil war was
ushered in by explosions of popular anger against 'papists' and 'malignants' who were held to be responsible for the depression of trade and
the sufferings of the people, especially in the badly hit cloth manufactu-
ring districts. Thus at Colchester in Essex in August 1642 a rumour
spread through the town that Sir John Lucas was preparing to send
horses and arms to the king. The mayor set a watch on Sir John's
house and at midnight some horses were seen coming out of a back-gate
The mayor reported to parliament what happened next:

> Presently word was brought into the town that there were a hundred
> men in arms at Sir John's. The drums thereupon beat up, the town
> got into an uproar, and the trained band and volunteers presently
> beset the house. There are gathered together, besides the bands,
> 5000 men, women, and children, which I feared might do some hurt.
> I therefore, being accompanied by some other justices and aldermen,
> made proclamation in several places where the tumults were, at one
> o'clock in the night and several times since, charging the people to
> depart. They however regarded us no more than they do a child, and then
> we charged the bands to keep careful watch about the house. This they
> did until daylight, and then the rude sort of people broke into Sir
> John's house [and seized his horses and arms]. Nothing would
> satisfy these tumultuous people but that Sir John Lucas, his mother,
> and his servants should be committed. I therefore desired Sir John
> to go to my house for safety, and he and his lady mother and his
> sister went there. When the people knew that they were not committed,

they came in great numbers and told me to my face that they would pull down my house upon my head. Sir John, his lady mother and sister then went to the Moot Hall, in order to save my house. . . . The rude people do much abuse themselves and Sir John also in rifling his house, spoiling his goods, and carrying away his plate, money, books, boxes, writings and household stuff. They are come to such a head being a mixed company of town and country, that we know not how to quiet them. Believe we could not repress them if we had five trained bands, unless they were killed.[32]

The House of Commons sent the two M.P.s for Colchester, Sir Thomas Barrington and Harbottle Grimston, to endeavour to restore order. They found that the people had risen throughout Essex and Suffolk and attacked the houses of papists and malignants, who were the causers of the distractions of the kingdom, 'and were the occasion that they, their wives and children were brought into great want and extremity, (by the great decay of trading). . .'.[33]

Arthur Wilson, steward to the Earl of Warwick, went to the rescue of the Countess Rivers, a Catholic, whose seat was Long Melford House near Sudbury in Suffolk. He described how

a gentleman came posting from the Countess of Rivers to crave the protection of my lord's family . . . . So I was commanded to take some five men and a coach with six horses, to fetch the Lady Rivers. . . . With difficulty I passed through the little villages of Essex, where their black bills and coarse examinations put us to divers demurs. . . . When I came to Sudbury in Suffolk, within three miles of Long Melford, not a man appeared till we were within the chain. But then they began to run to their weapons, and, before we could get to the market place, the streets swarmed with people. I came out of the coach, as soon as they took the horses by the heads, and desired that I might speak with the mayor, or some of the magistrates, to know the cause of this tumult, for we had offended nobody. The Mouth cried out, this coach belongs to the Lady Rivers, and they are going to her. (And indeed the gentleman, who came along with me, was known by some of the town.) And some, who pretended to be more wise and knowing than the rest, said, that I was the Lord Rivers. And they swarmed about me, and were so kind as to lay hold on me. But I calmly entreated those many hundreds which encircled me, to hear me speak; which before they had not patience to do, the confusion and noise was so great. I told them, I was steward to the Earl of

Warwick, a lover of his country, and now in the parliament's employment; that I was going to Bury St Edmunds about business of his, and that I had letters in my pockets (if they would let any of the magistrates see them) which would make me appear to be a friend and an honest man. This said, the Mouth cried out, Letters, Letters! The tops of the trees, and all the windows, were thronged with people who cried the same. At last the mayor came crowding in with his officers; and I showed him my letters (which indeed I had received a little before from my lord, and, fearing the worst, thought the bringing them might be an advantage to my passage). The Mayor's Wisdom said, he knew not my lord's hand; it might be, and it might not. And away he went, not knowing what to do with me, nor I to say to them ... till Mr Man, the town clerk (whose father was my lord's servant) saw me at a distance. . . . He told the mayor and the people, I was the Earl of Warwick's steward: and his assurance got some credit with them. And so the great cloud vanished. But I could go no further to succour the Lady Rivers. For I heard, from all hands, there was so great a confusion at Melford, that no man appeared like a gentleman, but was made a prey to that ravenous crew. So my lady's gentleman, Mr Man and myself took horse (leaving the coach at Sudbury) and went a bye-way to Sir Robert Crane's, a little nearer Melford, to listen after the countess. Sir Robert told us, that she had in her own person escaped to Bury St Edmunds; and so was gone to London. But he was forced to retain a trained band in his house (although he was a parliament man) to secure himself from the fury of that rabble, who threatened him, for being assistant to her escape.[34]

Her house at Long Melford, wrote John Rous,

was defaced; all glass broken, all iron pulled out, all household stuff gone, all ceilings rent down or spoiled, all likely places digged where money might be hidden, the gardens defaced, beer and wine consumed and let out (to knee-deep in the cellar), the deer killed and chased. . . . Sir Francis Mannocke's house was pillaged of all goods; (and, as is said, not his writings spared, which he craved, but were torn, nor his dogs). Also Mr Martin's house pillaged. Doctor Warren's house was rifled for his 'Gods', and a great many set about the market cross, termed 'young ministers'. Him they huffed and shuffed about, but (as is said) hurt not otherwise, though he say they took money from him. This insurrection scareth all the malignant party.[35]

'This fury', observed Wilson, 'was not only in the rabble, but many of
the better sort behaved themselves as if there had been a dissolution of all
government; no man could remain in his own house without fear, nor
be abroad with safety.'[36]

The people set out to disarm papists and supporters of the king, but
they transferred their rage to unpopular landlords like Sir John Lucas,[37]
(hence the concern of the mobs to destroy 'writings', which were the
records of leases and the obligations of the tenants), and to the nobility
and gentry as such – 'no man appeared like a gentleman, but was made a
prey to that ravenous crew'. Fear of papists fusing with anger over the
trade depression released latent hostility to the ruling class. Clarendon
believed that the hatred of tradesmen and artisans for the nobility and
gentry was 'natural' and that it came into the open at this time.[38]
William Lilly observed that in London during the winter of 1641–2,
when fear of papists was reaching a climax and trade was rapidly
declining, 'the present hatred of the citizens was such unto Gentleman
especially courtiers, that few durst come into the city, or if they did,
they were sure to recieve affronts and be abused'.[39] Hatred for the
nobility and gentry expressed itself in attacks on 'cavaliers', a term for
gentlemen. Clarendon described 'the fury and license of the common
people, who were in all places grown to that barbarity and rage against
the nobility and gentry, (under the style of cavaliers,) that it was not
safe for any to live at their homes who were taken notice of as no votaries
to the parliament'.[40] And after the first battle of the civil war Charles I
accused the parliamentarians of raising 'an implacable malice and hatred
between the gentry and commonalty of the kingdom, by rendering all
persons of honour, courage, and reputation, odious to the common
people, under the style of cavaliers, insomuch as the high-ways and
villages have not been safe for gentlemen to pass through without
violence or affronts. . .'.[41]

Fear of papists, depression of trade and antagonism of classes combined to produce the situation in which county after county was torn
apart in civil war, despite the efforts of most of the gentry to keep the
peace. In Somerset the Marquis of Hertford and some of the leading
gentry of the county made their headquarters at Wells and tried to
raise men for the king. But they were forced to flee by a huge crowd of
men and women, armed with 'pitchforks, dungpeeks, and such like
weapons, not knowing (poor souls) whom to fight against, but afraid
they were of the papists'.[42] The Marquis believed that the people
were roused against the royalist nobility and gentry 'by false and

scandalous suggestions' that their intention was 'to enthrall the people
and to take away great part of their estates...'.[43] According to Clarendon
the people believed that they were to be made 'no better than slaves to
the lords, and that there was no way to free and preserve themselves
from this insupportable tyranny than by adhering to the Parliament,
and submitting to the ordinance for the militia, which was purposely
prepared to enable them to resist these horrid invasions of their liberties'.[44] It was alleged that Lord Poulett, one of the greatest landlords in
the county and a prominent supporter of the king, had said that no
yeoman ought to have more than £10 a year,

> and withall manifested to this purpose, though not perhaps in these
> words, that when the power should be totally on their side, they
> shall be compelled to live at that low allowance, notwithstanding
> their estates are gotten with a great deal of labour and industry. . . .
> The people did not take this speech as only directed to the yeomen,
> but to all men under the degree of a gentleman, or such whom he
> will allow to be so. . . .[45]

Farmers refused to follow their landlords into the royalist camp and
offered to pay their rents to parliament instead.[46] The yeomen and
clothiers, and the whole 'middle rank' of people in Somerset, as well as
the 'poorer sort', turned to parliament to defend them against the
royalist nobility and gentry.[47]

The West Riding of Yorkshire similarly rose in the winter of 1642–3
in fear of 'burning, disarming, imprisoning, killing' by papists and
cavaliers.[48] The Fairfaxes put themselves at the head of this rising, and
the situation was seen by the son of a family of clothiers in these terms:

> . . . insomuch as all trade and business was interrupted and laid aside,
> Lord Fairfax and Sir Thomas his son, came to Leeds and those parts
> to list soldiers; my brother Samuel went amongst the rest, but he
> came over to Goodgreave to take his leave of my mother, uncles, and
> friends. What entreaty and persuasions there was to keep him at
> home, but could not prevail. My mother went along with him a
> quarter of a mile, and I with her, as children used to do; she besought
> him with tears not to go; I remember his words, 'Mother', saith he,
> 'Pray be content; if I stay at home I can follow no employment, but
> be forced to hide myself in one hole or another, which I cannot
> endure; I had rather venture my life in the field, and, if I die, it is
> in a good cause'; so most honest men thought in those times, when

hundreds of Protestants were daily murdered in Ireland, and fearing the same tragedy would be acted in England. . . .[49]

So unemployment and fear of papists combined to produce the rising in the West Riding.

The distrust of the intentions of the royalist nobility and gentry that provoked the peasants and artisans of Somerset was matched by the distrust of the intentions of the common people that boiled up in the minds of many of the nobility and gentry, parliamentarian as well as royalist. The willingness of the Fairfaxes to lead the rising of the clothiers in the West Riding shocked other leading parliamentarian gentry in Yorkshire such as Sir Hugh Cholmley and Sir John Hotham. The latter's son wrote to the royalist Earl of Newcastle:

> My Lord, there is one thing more, which I fear much, that if the honourable endeavours of such powerful men as yourself do not take place for a happy peace, the necessitous people of the whole kingdom will presently rise in mighty numbers and whosoever they pretend for at first, within a while they will set up for themselves, to the utter ruin of all the nobility and gentry of the kingdom. I speak not this merely at random, the west part of this county affords mighty numbers of them, which I am very confident you will see necessitied and urged to rise in far greater bodies than these . . . and if this unruly rout have once cast the rider, it will run like wildfire in the example through all the counties of England.[50]

Cholmley and the Hothams stood aside while the Earl of Newcastle crushed the rising in the West Riding, and soon after they deserted from the parliamentarian cause. In increasing numbers moderate nobility and gentry began to side with the king out of fear of social revolution and in defence of the social order, but others were cowed into collaborating with parliament, while a few radical gentry seized the opportunity to ride to power on the backs of the mob.[51]

Popular identification of the royalists with 'papists', 'cavaliers', 'malignant nobility and gentry', and defence of the existing social order, meant that the emerging hostility towards the ruling class flowed into the parliamentarian party. The people accepted leaders from among the nobility and gentry, as any group accepts allies from dissident members of the group that it opposes, and regarded such leaders as patriots, protestants and defenders of the people, rather than as just their social superiors. But it was an uneasy alliance, filled with suspicion and distrust on both sides,[52] and it was touch-and-go whether the currents of hostility towards the ruling class which flowed into and carried along the parliamentarian party would not sweep away the existing social order.[53]

SHORT BIBLIOGRAPHY

Narratives

S. R. Gardiner, *History of England*, 10 vols (1884), vol. ix (1639–41), vol. x (1641–2).

C. V. Wedgwood, *The King's Peace 1637–1641* (1955); *The King's War 1641–1647* (1958).

Background

M. A. Judson, *The Crisis of the Constitution* (New Brunswick, N.J., 1949).

J. W. Allen, *English Political Thought 1603–1660* (1938), vol. i (1603–4).

William Haller, *The Rise of Puritanism* (New York, 1938).

Special Studies

D. Brunton and D. H. Pennington, *Members of the Long Parliament* (1954).

Valerie Pearl, *London and the Outbreak of the Puritan Revolution* (Oxford, 1961).

Margaret James, *Social Problems and Policy During the Puritan Revolution* (1930).

NOTES

1. *Lord Montagu of Beaulieu MSS*, HMC, liii (1900) 129–30; *The Letters and Journals of Robert Baillie*, ed. D. Laing, 3 vols (Edinburgh, 1841) i 353; *Cowper MSS*, ii, HMC, xxiii (1888) 282–3.

2. J. L. Sanford, *Studies and Illustrations of the Great Rebellion* (1858) pp. 373–5, quoting the journal of Sir Simonds D'Ewes; John Rushworth, *Historical Collections*, pt v, "The Tryal of Thomas Earl of Strafford", 2nd ed. (1700) pp. 744–5.

3. Baillie, op. cit. i 352; Nehemiah Wallington, *Historical Notices of Events Occuring Chiefly in the Reign of Charles I*, ed. R. Webb, 2 vols (1869) i 244; *The Diurnall Occurrences or Dayly Proceedings*, 3 Nov 1640 – 3 Nov 1641 (1641) p. 93; *Lord Montagu of Beaulieu MSS*, p. 129.

4. Sanford, op. cit., pp. 373–5.

5. *Reliquiae Baxterianae*, ed. M. Sylvester (1696) pp. 28–9.

6. *A Great Discovery of a Damnable Plot at Ragland Castle* (1641).

7. *LJ* iv 439–40; *A Discovery of a horrible and Bloody Treason and Conspiracie* (1641); *England's Deliverance, Or, A Great Discovery* (1641).

8. *Portland MSS*, iii, HMC xxix (1894) 81–2; *Bridgewater MSS*, HMC, xxii (1888) 147; *Corporation of Bridgnorth MSS*, HMC, xiii (1885) 433–4; Baxter, op. cit., p. 29; Penry Williams, 'Government and Politics in Ludlow, 1590–1642', *Transactions of the Shropshire Archaeological Society*, lvi (3) (1960) 290–1.

9. Wallington, op. cit., i 279, 289, 290; *A Letter from Mercurius Civicus to Mercurius Rusticus* (1643), Somers's Tracts, iv 580–98; Sir Simonds D'Ewes, *Journal*, ed. W. H. Coates (New Haven. Conn., 1942) pp. 392–3; *Cal. S. P.*

Dom. 1641–3, pp. 245–6, 249; *Diurnall Occurrences: Or the Heads of Severall Proceedings in both Houses of Parliament,* 3 Jan–10 Jan 1642.

10. Wallington, op. cit., ii 1–2; D'Ewes, op. cit., p. 401; *A True Diurnall of the Last Weeks Passages in Parliament,* 10 Jan–17 Jan 1642; *Cal. S. P. Dom.* 1641–3, p. 254; *Calendar of State Papers Venetian,* xxv 280–1; Edward, Earl of Clarendon, *The History of the Rebellion,* ed. W. D. Macray, 6 vols (Oxford, 1888) i 510–12.

11. *The Diurnall Occurrances in Parliament,* 17 Jan–24 Jan 1642; *A Perfect Diurnall of the Passages in Parliament,* 24 Jan–31 Jan 1642; *A True Diurnal Occurrences or Proceedings in the Parliament,* 24 Jan–31 Jan 1642.

12. Wallington, op. cit., ii 9.

13. *Buccleuch MSS,* i, HMC, xlv (1899) 290.

14. Wallington, op. cit., ii 11, 12, 15; *A Perfect Diurnall of the Passages in Parliament,* 14 Feb–21 Feb 1642.

15. *CJ* ii 412, 423; *LJ* iv 573; *Diurnal Occurences: Or, The Heads of the Proceedings in both Houses of Parliament,* 7 Feb–14 Feb 1642; *A Continuation of the True Diurnall of Passages in Parliament,* 7 Feb–14 Feb 1642; Wallington, op. cit., ii 9.

16. *Three Petitions. The One, Of the Inhabitants of the Towne of Colchester: The other Two, Of the County of Essex* (1642).

17. *The Clothiers Petition to His Majesty* (1642).

18. *LJ.* iv 573.

19. Ibid., pp. 536–7.

20. *A Continuation of the True Diurnall of Passages in Parliament,* 17 Jan–24 Jan 1642; *A Continuation of the True Diurnall Occurrences and Passages in both Houses of Parliament,* 21 Feb–28 Feb 1642; G. W. Johnson, *Memoirs of the Reign of Charles I,* 2 vols. (1848) ii 367–72; *The Humble Petition of the Clothiers, inhabiting in the Parish of Leeds, Vicarage of Halifax and other parts adjoining, in the County of York* (1642).

21. *Two Petitions of the Knights, Gentlemen, Freeholders, and other of the Inhabitants of the County of Hertford* (1642); *LJ* iv 575.

22. *Calendar of State Papers Venetian,* xxv 291.

23. *A True Copy of the Masterpiece of all those Petitions which have formerly been presented by the Mayor, Aldermen, and the rest of the Common Council of the City of London* (1642); *LJ* iv 534–5, 537–9.

24. *LJ* iv 523–4, 527, 530, 531, 532–3; *Cowper MSS* ii 304.

25. *LJ* iv 540–3; *A Speech Delivered at a Conference with the Lords, January 25. 1641. By John Pym Esq.*

26. *LJ* iv 544.

27. *The humble Petition of many thousand poor people, in and about the City of London* (1642); *The True Diurnall Occurrances or, The heads of the Proceedings of Both Houses in Parliament,* 31 Jan–7 Feb 1642; *Cowper MSS,* ii 306.

28. *LJ* iv 559; *Mr Hollis His Speech in Parliament on Monday the 31st of January* (1642).

29. *CJ* ii 407; *The True Diurnall Occurrances or, The heads of the Proceedings of Both Houses in Parliament,* 31 Jan–7 Feb 1642.

30. *To the Honourable the Knights, Citizens and Burgesses, in the Commons House of Parliament now assembled,* BM 669 f. 4 (55).

31. *LJ* iv 558–60.

32. *Braye MSS,* HMC, xv (1887) 146–7.

33. *A message sent to the Parliament from the Members of the House of Commons at Colchester* (1642); *CJ* ii 736–8, 740–1; *The Diary of the Rev. Ralph Josselin,* Camden Society, 3rd ser. xv (1908) p. 13.

34. Francis Peck, *Desiderata Curiosa* (1735) ii (12) 23–5.

35. *Diary of John Rous*, Camden Society, lxvi (1856) 121–2; John Rushworth, *Historical Collections* (1721) iv 680.

36. Peck, op. cit., ii (12) 23.

37. *LJ* iv 272, 285, 293, 307, 312, 313, 317, 322; *Lords MSS*, HMC, 4th report, i 86, 93, 94.

38. Clarendon, op. cit., ii 226, 464, iii 449.

39. William Lilly, *Monarchy or No Monarchy in England* (1651) 105–7.

40. Clarendon, op. cit., ii 318; *A Royalist's Notebook*, ed. F. Bamford (1936) pp. 105–6.

41. Edward Husbands, *An Exact Collection* (1642) pp. 649–50.

42. *A True and Exact Relation*, 19 Aug 1642, BM E. 112 (33).

43. *A Declaration Made by the Lord Marquis of Hertford* (1642).

44. Clarendon, op. cit., ii 295–6.

45. *A Memento for Yeomen, Merchants, Citizens, and all the Commons in England* (1642).

46. *Joyful News from Wells* (1642); *Special Passages*, 20 Sept–27 Sept 1642. Similarly in Cheshire, R. N. Dore, *The Civil Wars in Cheshire* (Chester, 1966) p. 19. Peasants who were in conflict with their lords tended to support parliament: B. G. Blackwood, 'The Lancashire Cavaliers and their Tenants', *Transactions of the Historic Society of Lancashire and Cheshire*, cxvii (1965); J. D. Hughes, 'The Drainage Dispute in the Isle of Axholme', *Lincolnshire Historian*, ii 1 (1954).

47. Clarendon, op. cit., ii 296, iii 78, 426, 449; and similarly in Gloucestershire, John Corbet, *An Historicall Relation of the Military Government of Gloucester* (1645).

48. 'Memoirs of Captain John Hodgson' *Original Memoirs Written During the Great Civil War* (Edinburgh, 1806) pp. 89–96.

49. 'Some Memoirs Concerning the Family of the Priestleys', *Yorkshire Diaries and Autobiographies in the Seventeenth and Eighteenth Centuries*, ii, Surtees Society, lxxvii (1883) 26–7.

50. *Portland MSS*, i, HMC xxix (1892) 87.

51. Christopher Hill, Oliver Cromwell, Historical Association Pamphlet G.38 (1958) pp. 11–13; *A Continuation of Certain Special and Remarkable Passages*, 5 Sept–9 Sept 1642; Sir Edward Walker, *Historical Discourses* (1705) pp. 271–2.

52. *A Copy of a Letter Writ from Serjeant Major Kirle* (1643); Lucy Hutchinson, *Memoirs of Colonel Hutchinson* (1848) p. 166.

53. I am grateful for the assistance I have received while writing this essay from Dr Christopher Hill, Dr R. Clifton and Dr I. J. Prothero.

2. The Rebels of 1642

D. H. PENNINGTON

THERE are some phrases and sentences so irresistibly attractive to writers of history that they appear, with minor variations, in an enormous range of books. Some classic favourites ('this was an age of transition'), having served for almost every time and place, slowly fall into disrepute. Others are tied to a single episode; and of these the hardiest may well be the bare statement of fact 'On August 22 Charles I raised his standard at Nottingham.' There is a good chance that it will be followed by the well-authenticated deduction 'The Great Civil War had begun.' Hardly anyone pauses at this dramatic point in the story to consider the significance of the ceremony of raising the standard. To Charles it was a symbolic and self-consciously antiquarian summons to his loyal subjects to perform their duty of aiding him in the crushing of his enemies. But standard-raising was at least as much the action of the feudal baron demanding the military service of his tenants, of the chieftain calling out his clansmen, and above all of the rebel proclaiming his resistance to the government and rallying support. Sir Thomas Wyatt had raised his standard at Maidstone in 1554; the Earl of Northumberland had made the same gesture of revolt in the north in 1569. In 1601 Essex, to his cost, had rejected the advice to leave the capital and set up a standard in Wales. Less than a year before the episode at Nottingham, Sir Phelim O'Neill had gathered behind a standard in Ireland the forces whose reported barbarities had been used to convince the English parliament of the existence of a huge Catholic conspiracy which the king's advisers were suspiciously slow to resist.

The symbolism on that stormy Monday afternoon could hardly have been more unfortunate for royal supporters. Manifestly this was not a monarch in his capital organising the defence of his realm against a minority of traitors: it was an anxious man on a hillside behind the ruinous castle of an insignificant county town, watched by a few hundred supporters and spectators. York, the recognised northern capital, would have made a plausible centre of royal authority; but the Yorkshire gentry had made it clear that their devotion to their king would be strengthened if he would go somewhere else. Lancashire and Wales, where royalism was thought to be stronger, both seemed more remote from the politically effective part of the country. The Trent might at least be a useful line in an unpredictable campaign. Like most of Charles's decisive moments, the standard-raising went badly wrong. In January he had stridden majestically into the House of Commons to shatter his opponents by arresting the five parliamentary leaders, and retreated in stammering confusion when he found they were not there. In April he had appeared in person to take charge of the town of Hull and its store of arms and ammunition. The gates were closed against him, and after a humiliating attempt to bargain with Sir John Hotham he had gone away. Now he had returned to Nottingham after abandoning without a blow the attempt to occupy Coventry. Though the intention to raise the standard had been announced well in advance, no one was prepared for a historic ceremony; and no one knew quite what to do.[1]

The standard was probably designed and painted in Nottingham – Rushworth claimed that it was like the streamers used in the Lord Mayor's show – and had been flown from a turret of the castle before Charles insisted on the formal 'raising'. Whether or not Clarendon was right in reporting that the standard blew down, it is clear that the solemn trumpet calls and the proclamation were pitifully ineffective. Hardly anyone responded to the summons to arms, even when the whole performance was repeated on the two following days. On the twenty-fifth the Earl of Southampton and Sir John Culpepper were sent to their respective Houses of Parliament with proposals for negotiation. Lords and Commons agreed that they would have nothing to say until Charles had not only withdrawn his accusations of treason against their members, but had taken down his standard.[2] But their public attitude to the king's action was still an ambiguous, indeed a nonsensical one. Only the death sentence itself more than six years later stated in plain terms the uncompromising view: 'The said Charles Stuart hath traitorously and maliciously levied war against the present Parliament and the people therein represented.'[3] In 1642, and throughout the war, M.P.s, legal draftsmen and pamphleteers were trying implausibly to reconcile the obvious facts with the long-established theories. It had been an essential part of their creed that they were demanding only a return to the past and would do nothing to break the continuity of the sovereign state on which the security of their status and property depended. However thin the fiction had worn, they could not admit the main fact on which the nature of the Civil War depended: a revolution in government had already taken place. Parliament had ceased to be a body that from time to time met at the king's behest, brought him the petitions and the subsidies of those of his people it represented, and gave – or occasionally withheld – its assent to the legislation devised by his ministers. It had become the effective ruler of the country. That was why Charles's rebel-like behaviour was more than a superficial parallel.

If we turn back to the writings and speeches of the earlier opponents of Stuart ways of exercising royal power, it is clear that they would not for a moment have accepted this as the logical, or the possible, culmination of their policies. Like their Elizabethan predecessors, they had defended, and tried with some success to increase, the area of state affairs on which parliament was entitled to express its views. They had asserted, with a lot of inconsistency and only partial success, the right of the Commons to control taxation. They had used the clumsy and to some extent fraudulent process of impeaching the king's ministers as a means of reversing policies they disliked. They had devised various methods of removing royal influence over their own proceedings.[4] But in the long and ponderous arguments about the nature of 'sovereignty' and the relations between the monarch, the law and the people they had not doubted that a great many functions must remain to the king and his ministers. In the 'harmony' that was the mark of the successful constitution, the most exalted and unchallengeable power might be that of the king in parliament. The king out of parliament would still have plenty to do.

It has sometimes puzzled admirers of Sir John Eliot that when his opposition in the parliaments of the 1620s finally landed him in the Tower he occupied some of his time in writing a treatise – a highly derivative one – hardly less austere in its defence of royal sovereignty than James I himself had been.[5] *De Iure Majestatis* was certainly very different in tone from the speeches and the resolutions in parliament. But it was not in principle incompatible with them. 'Upon good occasion of state' the king could and must exercise ultimate authority. No one went as far in claiming supremacy for parliament as Sir Edward Coke in claiming it for the Common Law: 'The king hath no prerogative but what the Law of the Land allows him.' Round the term 'prerogative' an immense amount of technical and antiquarian argument had developed. 'High', 'special' or 'absolute' prerogative could be distinguished in a variety of tortuous explanations from 'ordinary' prerogative. Sometimes the emphasis was on a right to act in emergency, sometimes on the necessity to do whatever 'the common good' required. The parliamentarians did not deny either of these outright. One of the clearest statements of theory on 'sovereignty' was that made by James Whitelock in 1610.[6] The sovereign's power was twofold, 'the one in Parliament as he is assisted with the consent of the whole state, the other out of Parliament . . . guided merely by his own will'. And the power of the king in parliament could always overrule his power outside it. There were moreover some functions which 'belong to the King only in Parliament' – principally those that involved taking away the property of his subjects. Others, 'by the use and practice of the Commonwealth', it was accepted that he exercised alone.

The conflict went far deeper than theories of the constitution. As the system of Court patronage and venality grew, and the inner circle of royal advisers seemed further and further removed from the well-established community of gentry, lawyers and merchants represented in the Commons, bargains between parliaments and the royal council were harder to reach. But there was no steady progress towards a total breakdown of 'harmony'. In 1624 parliament appeared to be working in happy collaboration with Buckingham himself, voting subsidies, legislating on a wide range of national and local topics, debating foreign policy with the approval of James – 'seeing that of my princely fidelity you are invited thereto'. Though the relaxation of tension was largely an accidental product of the twist of Buckingham's irresponsible policy that made the Spanish supporters at Court accuse him of selling out to the opposition, it was the kind of accident that could easily happen again. Even the angry parliament of 1628–9 did not give Charles much cause for alarm. The royal assent to the Petition of Right made, as was soon apparent, little difference to the practical working of the government. Nor was it much sign of courageous determination to resist when members sat on the Speaker to ensure the reading of yet another set of resolutions and then went quietly home at the king's command.

What would happen next no one was eager to predict. It is far too readily assumed, in the light of the events of 1640, that the Personal Rule was an interlude doomed to end as soon as the treasury had to face the strain of a war. There was no inherent economic or administrative reason why the assorted non-parliamentary forms of taxation which enabled the royal government to survive in the years of peace should not have been expanded. In Europe there seemed to be many signs that the days of representative Estates were coming to an end. Richelieu did not find it necessary to summon the Estates General; and though some of the crushing war taxes of Gustavus Adolphus were granted by the Riksdag, others, in face of their ineffectual protests, were not.[7] The Cortes of Castile and Aragon had likewise ceased to play an important part in the shaky economy of the Spanish crown. The decisive moment in England that blighted royal absolutism in its infancy came not with the Scottish wars but in 1637, when respectable and unimpassioned gentlemen began to act unlawfully in their opposition to the demands of the government. Why it should have been ship-money that produced the change from the protests of a small minority to direct action by a steadily growing mass of taxpayers is not obvious. As royal taxes went, this one had many merits. Attempts to prove that the money was not really used for the navy at all were unconvincing: it was dealt with outside the old Exchequer routine, on the 'Declared Accounts' system which gave the Council direct control over it, and went straight to naval funds. The assessments were comparatively realistic, and related to separate estimates of the wealth of each county and town. The first year's receipts from the whole country came very close to the estimated amount. There was even provision for lenient treatment of those whose estates were heavily burdened.[8]

The success of the tax, and the zeal with which the Council watched its progress, were of course added reasons for opposition to it on the part of those who were anxious to see parliamentary control over finance restored. A new assessment, whether or not it was a fair one by any standards, was more distressing than the familiar absurdities of the subsidy books. The sheriff may have been chosen as the official responsible for the county's collection in the hope that this would diminish resentment. But it was a post whose importance had declined, and it was now held, briefly and without much enthusiasm, by a succession of gentry who were within the ruling circle of county society but were seldom its leaders. The great objection of the legally minded organisers of resistance was that unlike all the other forms of royal money-raising this was a tax essentially the same as those that had been recognised as being granted only by parliament. As St John put it at Hampden's trial, a parliamentary grant preserved 'that fundamental propriety which the subject hath in his land and goods' – on the manifestly unrealistic grounds that 'each subject's vote is included in whatever is there done.'[9] The finely balanced arguments on each side were far less significant than the fact that the man on trial for his defiance of the royal government was neither a notorious political malcontent nor an emotional puritan. He was not even venting any personal or family ill-will towards the Court or the county establishment. John Hampden was the most improbable of rebel leaders. His virtues as a figurehead were his respectability, his wealth and his widespread connections inside Buckinghamshire and beyond it. The trial, originally the agreed setting for a public debate between lawyers, became a piece of publicity of exactly the kind needed to push the propertied classes gently towards refusal. Hampden's slowly won supporters were men who believed in a system of law the main purpose of which was the protection of property. If the Crown failed to uphold what they regarded as legality, a point was reached where they would uphold it even against the Crown itself. By 1640 less than a quarter of the ship-money demanded was being paid.

Once the active resistance had begun, everything seemed to move in its favour. In the absence of parliament, a great variety of centres for discussion and consolidation appeared. The trading companies – Saybrooke, Providence Island, Massachusetts Bay – that were notoriously the preserve of opposition leaders, the puritan congregations, the outstanding gentry 'connections' in the south-west and in the eastern counties have been thoroughly investigated.[10] Below the level of the central political leadership nearly every county seems to have developed a group, or separate groups, of gentry whose grievances and resentments were gradually aligned in opposition to the Court. The Laudian Church provided one stimulus to resistance. The one nation-wide organisation that had set itself to inculcate passive obedience to authority went just far enough in its 'popish innovations' and its inquisitorial behaviour to build up anti-clerical, and in particular anti-episcopal, feeling among people with little positive inclination towards puritan doctrine. Revelations of popery at Court and among officers of the army had enough foundation to make the wildest rumours plausible. The wars with Scotland might easily have been a disaster for the opposition. Political causes seldom benefit from association with a national enemy, especially one that is carrying out a victorious invasion. But the great majority of parliamentary supporters were at a fairly safe distance from the northern border. The Scots were a less immediate threat than the clumsily managed conscript armies that were supposed to repel them. The government's handling of the peace negotiations was a safe topic for complaint. In any case the main effect of the wars was to produce, at exactly the moment when the opposition was ready to broaden its attack, a new parliament and a new chief minister against whom the hatred of 'thorough' could be concentrated.

Strafford was in some ways a better victim than Buckingham had been. As a renegade from the parliamentary cause he was a natural target for personal retribution. Though his absence in Ireland had made him less directly responsible for the sins of the royal government, it also meant that he had few friends ready to strike a bargain to save him. For popular consumption, the vague charges against him ('. . . laboured and endeavoured to breed in his Majesty an ill opinion of his subjects . . . an intention and endeavour to ruin and destroy his Majesty . . .') and the scandalous phrases attributed to him ('. . . an army in Ireland which he might employ to reduce this kingdom . . . no good would be done till some of the aldermen were hanged up . . .') were more effective than legally demonstrable offences.[11] For the opposition lawyers the trial of Strafford was a humiliating defeat. The humiliation for Charles when he surrendered to the demand for his assent to the Bill of Attainder was greater still. What was not so apparent, even to Pym in his brilliantly managed programme, was that the trial was a further stage in the movement of the opposition towards taking over the functions of government. Even the Short Parliament in the spring of 1640 had been primarily an old-style opposition body, denying the subsidies rashly demanded by the Council. A year later the House of Commons refused to accept that failure to prove that Strafford had offended against the law meant that it had no means of overthrowing him. Repellant though the Act of Attainder was in terms of justice to an individual or of constitutional efficiency, it was a decisive step towards ministerial responsibility.

The work of the Long Parliament in 1641 has usually been seen mainly as a succession of statutes demolishing the legal apparatus of royal absolutism. Most of the constitutional legislation could more or less truthfully advertise itself as a return to the old order: 'Whereas by the laws and statutes of this realm . . .', 'Whereas by the Great Charter many times confirmed in Parliament . . .', 'Whereas by Act of Parliament made in the first year of the late King Edward III . . .'.[12] The destruction of the Prerogative Courts could not in itself make any vital difference to the working of royal government. Star Chamber was hated because it enforced, efficiently and sometimes brutally, the social and economic policies of 'thorough'; but it was not an indispensable part of the machinery. Ship-money was declared illegal only after it had ceased to be collected, and knighthood fines only when they could no longer be more than a very minor source of revenue. The statutes were important less for their direct effect than as demonstrations of the king's

surrender to parliamentary authority. The only crucial piece of legislation was the very brief enactment, drafted – according to Clarendon's
well-known account of it[13] – in less than an hour and put through as an
appendage to Strafford's attainder, which compelled the king to surrender his right of dissolving parliament. This was one part of a change
in the whole character of parliament far more revolutionary than anything that had been done to the law-courts or the church. Another part
was the increase in the amount of time M.P.s devoted to their work.
The Commons, which even in the 1620s had usually met for three or
four hours at most in the mornings and then adjourned, now accepted –
with some occasional grumbling – that an afternoon sitting was normal
and that from time to time it would be proposed that candles should be
brought and the sitting continue into the night. Committees were
sometimes summoned for 7 a.m. to get through their work before the
House met. The Lords, though notably less enthusiastic for long hours,
found their own work extended too. Parliament was no longer a body of
strangers from remote places who were summoned and sent away at
unpredictable intervals: it was as continuous a part of the government
as the Council or the Treasury.

From the earliest days of the Long Parliament the 'governing' element
in its work developed side by side with the 'opposing' one. It was
accepted that subsidies, which the parliaments of the twenties monoton-
ously postponed even when they did not refuse them outright, would
have to be voted quickly, and that while high indignation was expressed
about illegal collection of Tunnage and Poundage, an immediate
arrangement with the farmers of the customs would be necessary to
make sure the revenue continued to be paid over. Parliament alone
could ensure further loans from the City; and over all these funds it
intended to exercise a far more effective control than had ever been
attempted before. The armies in the north soon found that they now
had two masters, parliament and the Council. In January 1641 the Army
Treasurer, Sir William Uvedale, assured his deputy that 'the Parliament
is slow, but they will certainly pay all at last'. Sir Jacob Astley observed
that 'the Parliament has not been acquainted with the way to pay armies'
and that in the Lower House especially there were few who 'know the
course thereof'. By the spring Uvedale was discovering how to exploit
the situation to ease his own problems in distributing inadequate funds.
The pay that was to be handed over to Colonel Vavasour on the
Warrant of the Lord-General 'must come out of the King's money, yet
you must so carry the matter that he may think it comes out of the

Parliament money, to prevent the importunity of others'. And Matthew
Bradley suggested to him that if the various warrants could be kept until
accounts were finally made up 'we may place them upon either the King
or the Parliament as we shall see cause'.[14]

Parliament's dealings with the army were mainly through the committee that had been set up to examine 'the state of the King's army',
the means of paying it, and the condition of the northern counties –
normal enough parliamentary activities.[15] Some of its members were
experienced soldiers, others were leading politicians such as Holles and
Hampden. Uvedale himself was a member, though he was often absent
on his official duties. Gradually it extended and changed its functions.
It got authority to 'treat' with the Lord-Commissioners who were
handling negotiations with the Scots. To make possible the payment of
arrears, a general muster and a proper list of names were needed, and it
was agreed that this should be organised by a body appointed partly by
the Commissary-General and partly by the Yorkshire M.P.s. Orders
proposed by the committee were sent in the name of both Houses direct
to the commanders in the north. Officers began to send reports to the
Speakers of the Lords and Commons, and were sometimes summoned to
give an account of their activities. The tone of communications from the
Commons changed significantly: at first they were still prepared to
'entreat some honourable persons about this chair' – the familiar term
for Privy Councillors in the House – to convey their proposals to the
commander-in-chief. Before long they simply resolved that the House
'holds it fit that orders be sent . . .'.[16]

The army was only one of many spheres in which this rapid invasion
by parliament of the administration took place. The navy experienced
much the same change in the source from which decisions came;
commerce, the punishment of Catholic recusants, and the affairs of
Ireland (even before the rebellion there) were among the others. There
was nothing new in strong parliamentary concern with such topics; and
the change in attitude was so indeterminate that it was impossible for a
royal government that was making one surrender after another in
matters of legislation to put up much resistance to this development. It
was not of course carried out smoothly or without political animosity.
Within the House of Commons there were more and more manœuvres
to capture control of the powerful committees, to set up rival committees
that could encroach on the sphere of influence of older ones, to preserve
the sole decision-making power in the Houses themselves. On the whole
Pym's 'party' organisation proved well able to defeat both the root-and-

branch puritans on the left and the advocates of caution and respect for the monarchy on the right. Not that the rivalries can be seen entirely in such terms: one of the features of the committee system most important in the eventual alignment of sides was the emergence of men whose interest in maintaining and extending their own administrative power became at least as strong a motive as political or religious theories. Robert Scawen, chairman of the Army Committee, had been a Straffordian when the vote on the Earl's fate was taken: he continued to sit in parliament, and to assert his influence on army affairs, after the execution of the king. Robert Pye and Lawrence Whittaker were two courtiers and experts in the service of the royal government who became leading parliamentary committee-men and kept their seats throughout the war.[17] How many lesser men were encouraged by their first taste of authority in central government to remain loyal to the parliamentary cause there is obviously no means of knowing.

It was very difficult for Charles and for anyone in the Court circle to make sense of the behaviour of Pym and his allies. Even though the attack on Strafford had been extended to Finch, Windebank and Laud, there had been no suggestion that the object was to overthrow the power of 'counsellors' as such. Some, it seemed to be admitted, were more evil than others. By the autumn of 1641 it looked as though power was held by Pym, Hampden, Holles and the rest while office still belonged to such men as Edward Nicholas, who in November received Windebank's place as Secretary, Sir Edward Herbert as Attorney-General, and the leading member of the Council, the Earl of Bristol. The natural assumption of the king was that his prominent opponents were seeking office for themselves, and that their ranks could be split by some skilful bargaining with the places which parliament's impeachments and threats fortunately put at his disposal. There was certainly nothing improbable in such an idea. During Strafford's trial the Earl of Bedford appears to have tried to negotiate an agreement by which in return for sparing Strafford's life Pym should become – along with Bedford himself – one of the principal office-holders in a new government. In the summer Charles was disposed to refuse any suggestions that he should tolerate Pym and Hampden as ministers, but was willing enough to take on Falkland and Hyde. During 1641 eight peers who had been in greater or less degree opponents of royal policy were added to the Council; Lord Saye and Sele, one of Pym's prominent associates in the 1630s, acquired the profitable post of Master of the Court of Wards, Oliver St John became Solicitor-General, Essex was made Lord

Chamberlain.[18] The elder Vane remained until the end of the year the other Secretary. The line between the king's government and the parliament that looked so firm in the Commons was a much more flexible one from the Council's point of view.

Links of this kind between the parliamentary and the royal governing institutions were not enough to mitigate the strains that such a situation involved. Whatever compromises might have been possible on the remaining political and religious questions, the division of power that had developed could not continue for long without some major clash. It was one of Pym's very few failures to keep the progress of parliament's demands firmly under his control and to plan every move far ahead when he was caught unprepared by the need to ensure complete control over the suppression of the Irish Rebellion. The rising of the Irish Catholics in October 1641 was yet another piece of well-timed good fortune for the parliamentary leaders. Like such minor episodes as the 'Army Plots' in England, this unexpected event was exploited with superb and unscrupulous skill. Here at last was the visible proof of the great myth of the parliamentary cause – that there existed a world-wide conspiracy by the forces of Antichrist, with the Pope and the Spanish king at their head, to overthrow Protestant civilisation, the security of property and all the laws and liberties that had been so resolutely defended. Tales of massacre, rape and plunder were supplied to the House of Commons with a genuine horror that did not diminish appreciation of their convenient effect on the waverers. It was not necessary to offer any direct evidence of complicity with the rebels at the English Court, or to make any treasonable accusations that Charles himself was not anxious to suppress the rising. It was enough to stress that known favourers of papists were still to be found among the king's advisers. But the provision of an army to put down the Irish rebels and of the money to pay it raised, in a more dangerous form, the same difficulties of divided control that had been experienced by the commanders in the north. If there was any truth at all in the suspicions about the attitude of the king's counsellors to the rebellion, it would be folly to give them even partial control over the forces to be sent there.

A further complication was that Charles was now in Scotland, and obtained from the Scottish parliament an offer to raise an army if the English would pay it. Arrangements would have to be entrusted to commissioners sent, as was regularly happening, from parliament to the king. It was for them that Pym proposed, apparently on the spur of the moment, the original version of the fateful 'additional instruction' saying that parliament would not be bound to assist in suppressing the Irish rebellion unless the king would take such counsellors 'as might be approved by Parliament'. The suggestion that the Commons should actually refuse to carry out what was manifestly the most essential of all its duties – the defence of the realm against popery – gave a splendid opportunity to the growing number of members alarmed at the widening breach with the king. The matter had to be hastily shelved. When it came up again after fuller preparation it had been made not less but more drastic. 'If his Majesty should not be graciously pleased' to grant the request to remove his evil counsellors, then 'we should take such a course for the securing of Ireland as might likewise secure ourselves'.[19] Parliament, in other words, would take complete control of the armed forces required. There was no better test of where the ultimate power of government lay than that.

It was a remarkable demonstration of Pym's power to organise support that in its new form the 'instruction' won a safe majority – 151 to 110. But his following was clearly not what it had been in the days of the attack on Strafford. Hyde and Culpepper had insisted that it was parliament's duty to assist the king in the defence of his realm. Waller was forced to ask the pardon 'of the House and of Mr Pym' for a speech that hinted at a comparison between the parliamentary attitude and that of Strafford.[20] It was becoming very difficult to bridge the gap between those who wanted to change the policy of the king's Council and those who threatened to take away its powers. It does not appear to have been through any far-sighted planning that at this critical moment the Grand Remonstrance, which had been discussed sporadically ever since the beginning of the Long Parliament, was ready for final approval. The points of difference that emerged in the celebrated debate on 22 November were as a whole less decisive than the single dispute about the relations between parliament and ministers. The religious clauses had been argued out at length already; and the device of a synod of divines had been produced as part of the compromise that would gather the greatest possible range of support. But those who now broke away from Pym's political programme turned instinctively towards defence of episcopacy, in one form or another, and towards suspicion of what further religious changes might be attempted later. Even so, if the vote on the Remonstrance, with its frighteningly narrow majority of eleven votes in a crowded House, had been the end of the episode it might not have been beyond the skill of the Pym group to bring back most of those who had broken away. Charles could hardly have done less to attract them to his side. The breach was only made irreparable by the association of the parliamentary cause with popular agitation.

The year of the Ship-money trial and the beginning of the illegal resistance of property-owners was also a decisive moment in the development of a mass movement against the Stuart government and the Laudian Church. It was in 1637 that William Prynne, Henry Burton and John Bastwick were sentenced in Star Chamber to life imprisonment, to a fine of £5000 each, and to the loss of their ears – Prynne for the second time. They were all of thoroughly respectable origin: Prynne was a barrister, Burton a former Court chaplain dismissed for his puritanism, Bastwick a doctor of medicine. But they had the talent and inclination that Hampden totally lacked for publicising their martyrdom and appealing to the mass of Londoners. There was some reason for the ferocity of authorities who felt their own power to be bound up with that of the church. The pamphlets that were the immediate reason for the trial were not works of theological learning. *News from Ipswich*, *For God and the King*, *Flagellum Pontificis* and *The Litany of John Bastwick* attacked the Bishops in terms that ensured wide readership at a time when the output of the popular presses in London was already expanding quickly.[21] The suffering of the three in the pillory was turned into a highly successful demonstration. ('Methinks', said Burton, 'I see Mount Calvary with three crosses.') Though the prisoners after their ordeal were hastily taken to prisons in the Channel Islands and the Scillies, to get there involved overland journeys that became triumphal processions. In country towns as well as in the capital, hatred of 'thorough' had spread far down the social scale. Nor were these three the only ones whose fame grew in 1637. In December Laud's agents captured the 'notoriousest dispenser of scandalous books in the kingdom', John Lilburne. Sentencing Lilburne to be whipped through the streets and set in the pillory was another welcome gift of publicity to the enemies of Laud: he was reported to have distributed pamphlets during the punishment, as well as keeping up his colourful verbal denunciations until he was forcibly silenced.

From then on, the parliamentary cause was inescapably associated – sometimes to its embarrassment, often to its immediate advantage – with a popular resentment that exploded unpredictably into threats of mass violence. In the depressed years at the end of the decade, hostility to the tyranny of Bishops became on the whole less prominent than condemnation of the government as the originators of poverty and economic recession. What, if any, direct links existed between the crowds that demonstrated at Westminster on many of the crucial political occasions and the Pym organisation has not been discovered. But there is no doubt about the growing fear of disorder. It was this fear that came to a head in the Commons when the proposal to publish the Grand Remonstrance was brought forward at the end of the debate. 'I never dreamed', said Dering, until then a mild supporter of Pym, 'that we should remonstrate downwards, tell stories to the people, and talk of the king as a third person.'[22] Disputes about government were for men like him matters to be settled within the propertied nation, and must on no account threaten its monopoly of power. The quiet, stable settlement on the lines of an idealised Elizabethan constitution which they had assumed would replace the 'personal' government of Charles was looking less and less likely. The parliamentary leaders were seizing power as the allies of men whose views on the social hierarchy were not the ones assumed to be common ground among all those involved in the processes of government. It was another cogent reason for deserting the cause.

On 1 January 1642 Charles – or so it was reported[23] – offered Pym the post of Chancellor of the Exchequer. Pym's reply evidently left no doubt about his attitude: within a few hours the place had been given to Culpepper instead. At the same time Falkland, too, joined the inner-most circle of royal counsellors as Secretary. Hyde, no less firm in his change of loyalties, remained ostensibly an ordinary M.P.; but it was soon apparent that Charles had selected him as his principal adviser. There was some advantage in having in this position a man not under immediate attack in parliament and able to keep the king informed of everything that happened at Westminster, producing his well-framed drafts of the royal replies to the long succession of messages at the same time as they were sent. But it was only possible because governing had ceased to be the king's main concern. The take-over by parliament of the functions of the king's ministers was now accelerated. The Com-missioners of the Treasury continued to report to the king and to receive his instructions; but real financial power was held by parliament alone. Since the victory of parliamentary over royalist groups in the govern-ment of the City at the end of 1641,[24] London was putting its whole financial power at parliament's disposal, and was soon providing much of the administrative machinery to deal with the raising and spending of unprecedented sums of money. With Charles's departure, first for Windsor and then, in March, for York, it was impossible seriously to pretend that the country was still governed by the royal Council and

the royal office-holders. Lord Keeper Littleton had already shown
pardonable hesitation about what documents he ought to authenticate
with the Great Seal. In May he obeyed the order to take it to York –
after some severe brainwashing from Hyde. The loss was distressing to
some of the more legalistically minded M.P.s: in practice it made little
difference.

The ultimate test of any government's power was its ability to command the armed forces within its territory. The question of the Irish
army had shown that both sides recognised the importance of this while
the prospect of civil war was still remote. But the Irish problem had
itself done a great deal to make war in England conceivable – not just
because of its political and religious implications but because, then as at
any other time, wars only occur when the possibility of them has become
accepted. In 1629 no quarrel, however bitter, between king and parliament would have led to fighting because neither side held such a thing
to be within the bounds of practical politics. By 1642 armies on English
soil had become much more evident. There had been fighting on the
northern border already, and fighting in Ireland. The question of the
armed guard on parliament, and the defence of the Tower and the City
had been one of the topics of prolonged dispute. The determination of
both royal and parliamentary authorities to have armed force within
their own control merged rapidly into preparation for actual warfare.
The Militia Bill which completed the breaking off of all normal relations
between king and parliament was not in itself a drastic measure. When
it was carried as an 'ordinance of parliament' in March it claimed only
to be securing the safety of 'His Majesty's person, the Parliament, and
the Kingdom' from the wicked design of papists to stir up in England
'the like rebellion and insurrection' that had been seen in Ireland.[25]
And against such rebellion the county militias, amateur and ill-equipped
forces at best, were to be put under the control of Lord-Lieutenants
some of whom were new. It was a short step from this to the raising on
both sides of more mobile forces, modelled distantly on those in which
many English gentlemen had seen service abroad.

In May the little exodus from London began. The king's successive
summonses to the Peers, the Commons and various categories of office-
holders high and low to join him in the north faced each of them with the
inescapable choice of remaining in the capital, and in most cases continuing to do their job, obeying the order to abandon it for the unknown
conditions of service with Charles, or seeking some sort of passive
neutrality. The process of attempting to destroy the London govern-

ment was surprisingly slow.[26] It was not until February 1643 that the
Auditors of the Exchequer were officially ordered to attend at Oxford.
The king's greatest reluctance – shared by his enemies – was to interfere
with the legal system: only in November 1643 did he add the judges of
King's Bench and Common Pleas to those called on to sit in Oxford
instead of Westminster. By then there was a fairly well-equipped and
active administrative machine functioning in what had become a true
royalist capital. Most of the real courtiers – the men whose whole lives
were centred on the king's household – obeyed the summons without
undue delay. In the middle and even in the higher ranks of professional
administrative service a great many rejected the call. Neutralism, where
it was possible, might be more attractive than outright support of
parliament; but there was little feeling that their obvious duty was to
the king.[27]

Parliament would not even now admit that a revolutionary change
had taken place in the distribution of power. It could not conceive of the
king, the indispensable symbol of state authority, being in rebellion
against the real government. Consequently it was very difficult to explain
how His Majesty came to be leading an army against another that had
been raised by parliament's command. Two rather different versions of
the situation were used, more or less at random, in the preambles to the
parliamentary legislation. One was that 'an army, consisting of papists,
delinquents, and others, ill-affected persons to the Protestant religion
and the laws and liberties of this kingdom, have possessed themselves
of His Majesty's person and by colour of his authority have . . . in a
barbarous and inhuman manner wounded and plundered many of His
Majesty's most faithful subjects. . . .'[28] The other was that 'the King,
seduced by wicked counsel, hath raised an army and levied war against
his parliament.' As 'there is no probable way under God' to suppress
these ill-affected persons except 'by the army raised by the authority of
Parliament', it was necessary to legislate without His Majesty's consent.[29]
On the first theory the king was acting under duress and must be
rescued; on the second he was acting under a misapprehension and
might be talked out of it. The distinction might have had some relevance
to the question of peace negotiations, though Pym's technique with
these was on the whole to let them take their course and collapse of their
own accord. In any case the way was left open for Charles to resume his
functions, under whatever conditions could be imposed, when the ill-
affected persons were defeated. This was the point at which the claim of
the 'moderate' parliamentarians to have a realistic political programme

broke down. The celebrated interchange between Manchester and Cromwell in 1644[30] did not merely indicate the difference between 'peace party' and 'war party': it showed that at that point neither of them had a solution to the problem. In any conceivable circumstances Charles would continue to struggle and conspire against a settlement that left him without what he regarded as the powers of a king.

With better luck there might have been an easy way out of the difficulty. Charles I was almost the only English king before the nineteenth century to inherit and occupy the throne in circumstances which left not the slightest possibility of a rival claimant. He was in his forties, healthy, all too securely married to the Catholic queen who had already borne him three sons. In a situation like the Wars of the Roses or the French Wars of Religion the parliamentary armies would have been led not by so uninspiring an aristocrat as Essex but by a rival king. If James had left a plausible bastard, or if a secret marriage of Elizabeth I could have been unearthed to provide a Tudor claimant, there need have been no unconvincing slogans about fighting on behalf of king and parliament and no worries about what could be said if Charles were killed in battle. Acceptance of mixed monarchy in a sense agreed by Pym would have been the price for a throne. As it was, the problem in its changing forms still looked insoluble when Cromwell in 1657 came within an inch of being crowned.

The impossibility of grasping the idea of a rebel king lay behind many of the celebrated heart-searchings. In some ways it was easier for great noblemen to appreciate the situation than for peace-loving gentry. There was an aristocratic element in the parliamentary leadership with an outlook and aim not altogether the same as those of the politicians in the Commons.[31] If James Stanley, seventh Earl of Derby, was able and eager to raise his tenants and retainers in support of Charles, Algernon Percy, tenth Earl of Northumberland, did not feel that he was repudiating the assumptions of his family or his class in taking, for as long as he chose, the side of Pym. Ever since the exaggerated resentments aroused by the presence of Scots at the Court of James I, the feeling had existed among great families with little interest in constitutional theories that the monarchy was not what it had been in 'the late Queen's time'. The claim of parliamentary leaders that theirs was the side of conservatism seemed to many outside the immediate quarrels to be well-founded. There was certainly no rush of old or new peers to rally round the standard at Nottingham. Only when the alignments were slowly crystallised in each region and county did the tendency for the greatest families to take the royal side become apparent.

It was the war itself, with its threats of confiscation of estates and its new systems of local government, that brought to the surface the many-sided divisions in the landed communities. In these wider quarrels the distinction between rebel and non-rebel was a matter of propaganda rather than reality. Some families were drawn to the king's side by a connection with the Court and its patronage, or by religious or economic activities that would expose them to the wrath of parliament. Many found themselves on one side or the other as an almost accidental outcome of the local rivalries. What in one place was the side of con-servatism and respectability, in another could be that of the outsiders. The royalists had one clear advantage. For them the single aim was unquestioned: the men in power in London must be destroyed and the king put back on his throne. It was only within the parliamentary side that a truly revolutionary cleavage arose. But unity in wanting to see Charles back in his capital was only relevant if victory could be achieved: it had no answer to the question of how a compromise settlement might be reached. Though only a tiny minority of the original parliamentarians came to accept the fact, there was only one way in which a government – and a shaky government especially – could deal with a defeated rebel, even if he had once been their sovereign. On 30 January 1649 most of Charles's former subjects would no doubt have been glad to join him in revolt against the rule of the army and its allies. There was nothing they could do about it.

SHORT BIBLIOGRAPHY

M. A. Judson, *The Crisis of the Constitution* (1949).
F. D. Wormuth, *The Royal Prerogative* (1939).
J. H. Hexter, *The Reign of King Pym* (1941),
S. E. Thorne, *Sir Edward Coke* (1957).
C. V. Wedgwood, *The King's Peace* (1955) and *The King's War* (1958).
A. H. Woolrych, *Battles of the Civil War* (1961).
A. M. Everitt, *The Community of Kent and the Great Rebellion* (Leicester, 1966).
F. C. Dietz, *English Public Finance, 1558–1641* (New York, 1932).
W. Notestein, *The Winning of the Initiative by the House of Commons* (reprint, 1949).

NOTES

1. There is an account of the raising of the standard in A. C. Wood, *Nottinghamshire in the Civil War* (1937) ch. 3. The fullest contemporary descriptions are the pamphlets *Exceeding Good News from Nottingham* and *A True and Exact Relation of the Manner of His Majesty's setting up of the Standard* . . . .

2. Rushworth, *Historical Collections*, iii (1) 785.

3. S. R. Gardiner, *Constitutional Documents of the Puritan Revolution* (1890) p. 377.

4. See especially the account of the use of committees in W. Notestein, *The Winning of the Initiative by the House of Commons* (reprint, 1949) and D. H. Willson, *The Privy Councillors in the House of Commons* (1940). Later studies of this include M. F. Keeler, 'There are no remedies for many things but a Parliament' in *Conflict in Stuart England*, ed. W. A. Aiken and B. Henning (1960) and Lotte Glow, 'Committee Men in the Long Parliament' in *HJ* viii (1965).

5. See R. W. K. Hinton 'Government and Liberty under James I' in *Cambridge Historical Journal*, xi (1953).

6. The essential parts of it are quoted in J. P. Kenyon, *The Stuart Constitution* (1966) p. 70.

7. M. Roberts, *Gustavus Adolphus* (1953–8) ii 67–88.

8. M. D. Gordon, 'The Collection of Ship Money' in *TRHS*, 3rd ser. iv (1910).

9. Gardiner, *Constitutional Documents*, p. 114.

10. J. H. Hexter, *The Reign of King Pym* (1941); A. P. Newton, *The Colonising Activity of the Early Puritans* (1914).

11. Gardiner, *Constitutional Documents*, pp. 156–8; Kenyon, *The Stuart Constitution*, pp. 206–10.

12. Those quoted are the Triennial Act, the Act for the Abolition of Star Chamber, and the Act for the Limitation of Forests, in Gardiner, *Constitutional Documents*, pp. 144, 179, 192.

13. Clarendon, *History of the Rebellion*, iii, para. 208.

14. *Cal. S. P. Dom.* 1640–1, pp. 424, 440, 545, 553.

15. *CJ* ii 34.

16. *CJ* ii 39, 40, 70, 82.

17. G. E. Aylmer, *The King's Servants* (1961) p. 380.

18. Aylmer, *King's Servants*, p. 11.

19. Gardiner, *Constitutional Documents*, p. 199.

20. D'Ewes, *Journal*, p. 95.

21. S. R. Gardiner, *History of England* (1884) viii 227–8.

22. D'Ewes, *Journal*, pp. 186–7; Rushworth, *Historical Collections*, iii (1) 425.

23. Gardiner, *History of England*, x 127.

24. See the full account of this in Valerie Pearl, *London and the Outbreak of the Puritan Revolution* (1961).

25. C. H. Firth and R. S. Rait, *Acts and Ordinances of the Interregnum*, 3 vols (1911) i 1.

26. Aylmer, *King's Servants*, p. 410.

27. See the detailed analyses of allegiance in Aylmer, *King's Servants*, ch. 6 § ix.

28. Firth and Rait, *Acts and Ordinances*, i 97.

29. Ibid., p. 38.

30. 'If we beat the king ninety and nine times, yet he is a king still. . . .' quoted in Gardiner, *History of the Great Civil War* (1891–3) iii 59.

31. See the articles by Brian Manning, 'The Nobles, the People, and the Constitution' in *PP* no. 9, and V. S. Snow, 'The Earl of Essex and the Aristocratic Opposition' in *JMH* xxxii.

3. The Trial of Charles I

C. V. WEDGWOOD

THE Trial of Charles I is one of the most startling – perhaps the most startling – event of English history. It certainly astounded all Europe in 1649. 'The most horrible and detestable parricide ever committed by Christians' – in words such as these it was almost everywhere condemned. Only in some of the Swiss Protestant cantons does there seem to have been a favourable reception to the event.

Kings had been deposed and killed before. But this was the first time that a king had been arraigned under his title as king and in the name of his people. Three weeks before putting him on trial the House of Commons proclaimed that 'The people under God are the source of all just power.' They went on to the rather less convincing proposition that the remnant of the House of Commons elected eight years previously truly represented the people. The charge was drawn up against 'Charles Stuart, King of England' with the emphasis on his royal office. At the trial itself, the chief prosecuting Counsel asserted in Westminster Hall that he was acting 'on behalf of my clients the People of England'.

There was a fanatic resolution in the minds of the leaders (if not always in the minds of the secondary actors in this event) to show that no divinity hedged the position of a king, that he was nothing more than the highest officer of State, a steward appointed by and for the people, who could be called to account by them. 'We will cut off his head with the Crown on it', Cromwell is alleged to have said. 'With the Crown on it' – this was the novelty of the business. That a monarch should come to grief through deposition, should be deprived of his royal office and his sacred character, and subsequently done to death – that had happened a number of times. Edward II, Richard II, Henry VI and Mary Stuart had all died violent deaths only after deposition.

But Charles was tried and executed as king and his death was intended as an attack on the mystique of kingship itself. This was new in 1649. It was the work of a dominant group of officers in the Parliamentary Army led by Oliver Cromwell the Lieutenant-General and his son-in-law

Henry Ireton, seconded by such political Republicans as Colonel Edmund Ludlow and such religious fanatics as Colonel Thomas Harrison. They acted in conjunction with a small resolute republican group in the House of Commons, the Commonwealth men as they were called, of whom Harry Marten was the most significant. The more famous Harry Vane withdrew from the trial, although he supported it in principle, because he had been at Court in his youth and felt a natural embarrassment at sitting in judgement on a man whose bread he had eaten.

The king for his part was no less fanatical. He believed with immovable constancy that God had given him paramount authority over his subjects, to protect them and their liberties, but as *he* saw them not as *they* saw them. He could not, therefore, abandon his power or agree to its limitation without committing a sin against the ordinance of God. He could not recognise the so-called authority of the people, still less of the unprecedented Court set up to try him, because to do so would have been not only politically but morally wrong. Thus his trial presented, in its most dramatic form, a confrontation between two irreconcilable theories of government.

When the English Civil War broke out in the summer of 1642 nobody had any idea or desire that it should end in the trial and death of the king. Parliament had already curtailed his power by impeaching, executing or driving into exile his chief ministers and abolishing the Prerogative Courts which were the main instruments of his extra-parliamentary authority. They wished to secure, once and for all, two things: control over the armed forces and over the choice of ministers. They also in a more confused fashion wanted to become the arbiters of the country's religious beliefs and organisations. Once they had secured these powers they would cease to be merely an advisory body, as they had been under the Tudors, and would become the effective governing body of the nation.

Parliament fought the civil war to achieve these ends which they held to be morally good as well as politically advantageous. The king fought to prevent them doing so, because he regarded their aims as not only politically offensive but contrary to the Will of God who had given him sole authority. The war solved nothing, because parliament had assumed that when the king was defeated he would bow to the logic of defeat and accept their terms; but he could not do so. Defeated, he still refused their terms. He evaded the issue; he tried to play off the Scots against the English, parliament against the army; finally he engineered a new

Royalist rising coupled with an invasion from Scotland – the events known as the Second Civil War.

It is beside the point to accuse Charles of dishonesty in his dealings. Believing as he did, he was morally compelled to do all in his power to regain his authority. Any means he could find to outwit his opponents was therefore acceptable to him. But if he for his part was driven to extremes by his theory of kingship and his faith in it, they were driven to what they did by the sheer necessity of the political impasse in which they found themselves. As Cromwell put it, 'Providence and necessity' compelled them to exact a final reckoning from the king, because there was no other way of restoring peace and stability to England.

The Second Civil War of 1648 made the king's death inevitable. Consider the position of the ordinary men and women of England in the year 1648: they had had four years of civil war causing considerable loss of life, serious damage to agriculture and industry, grave loss and interruption of overseas trade, general insecurity, local famine and epidemic disease. Then, with the final defeat of the king's forces in 1646, came a blessed interval: peace once more; recovery began; men looked forward to something better. But after less than two years' interval the war was rekindled by the king and his supporters. Let us make no mistake about it. King Charles was not popular with the people of England in the year 1648.

The Parliamentary Army, with the Yorkshireman, Lord Fairfax, as Commander-in-Chief and the East Anglian, Oliver Cromwell, as Lieutenant-General of the Horse, was the angriest and most disillusioned group in the country. They had been at one time flattered and misled by the king into believing that he would make terms with them rather than with Parliament. The discovery that he had no such intention and the outbreak of a new war aroused their righteous wrath. At a meeting at Windsor in May 1648, just before they set out to quell the Royalists, the principal officers of the Army solemnly swore that when peace was restored they would 'call Charles Stuart, that man of blood, to an account for that blood he had shed and mischief he had done . . . to the Lord's cause and people of these poor nations'.

They then spent the summer effectively defeating the Royalists. By October the King's friends were totally dispersed. In late October and November various regiments in the Army put forward petitions for justice on all delinquents (on 'war criminals', as we should say today). They emphasised *all* delinquents, regardless of rank: that was the key phrase. Under this pressure and probably with the advice of Cromwell's son-in-law, Henry Ireton (as Cromwell was still engaged in reducing the last Royalist stronghold at Pontefract), Fairfax, the Commander-in-Chief, authorised a petition from the whole Army to Parliament on 20 November 1648. This asked openly and clearly that the King be brought to trial.

Parliament reacted without enthusiasm. A Presbyterian majority in the House still persisted in the illusory hope that the King might agree to a Treaty. They had opened negotiations with him in the place of his honourable captivity in the Isle of Wight. They shelved the petition from the Army. Thereupon the Army took the law into their own hands.

They seized the King in the Isle of Wight and imprisoned him closely in Hurst Castle on the mainland. They marched on Westminster, occupied the approaches to the House of Commons and on 6 December 1648 forcibly excluded from Parliament all those members known to be favourable to the treaty with the King. The House of Commons was thus reduced to about fifty members, either favourable to, or in fear of, the Army. Cromwell had personally nothing to do with this purging of Parliament. He reached London from the North on the following day, and gave his approval to the *fait accompli*.

It was this little remnant, derisively called 'the Rump' by a hostile pamphleteer, which voted the notable resolution that all authority under God derives from the people, and then added the not very convincing statement that they themselves were the true representatives of the people: thus authority belonged to them. It is easy to mock their presumption, but what Parliament represented, or had ever represented, the people at that time? This Rump was under the control of the Army, and the Army was a citizen Army, recruited from a wide cross-section of the entire people. It is arguable that the Army in 1648 was the nearest thing to a national popular assembly that England had yet seen.

The proclamation of their power on the part of the Rump was followed by an Act of Parliament (as they inaccurately called it, for the Lords refused to accept it) setting up a High Court of a hundred and thirty-five persons for one month for the special purpose of trying the King.

The King, who had been moved to Windsor under guard, received the news with his customary calm, but let it be known that he recognised no judge of his actions other than God who had entrusted his people to him by divine decree. Such was the direct and simple theory behind the lonely and, in the circumstances, heroic stand that Charles was to make at his trial for the rights and duties of kingship as he saw them.

The theory behind the actions of Cromwell and the regicides was

more complex. They appealed to natural law; the natural law of self-
defence which comes into operation when the life of a people is threatened and absolves them from allegiance to the ruler. This was not a new
doctrine. It had come into currency in the previous century and had
been used to justify the revolt of the Dutch against Philip II.

John Cook, the barrister who was chosen to conduct the prosecution
of the King, fervently appealed to this natural law. If a King would
destroy his people, he argued, it is unnecessary even to ask by what law
he is to die. A King is entrusted with the sword to protect his people;
if he uses it against them it is self-evident that he becomes a public
enemy. 'This law need not be expressed – that if a King become a
tyrant he shall die for it. 'Tis so naturally implied, as there needs no
law for eating and drinking which also is to preserve life.'

The natural law of self-defence then, was the first justification for
bringing the King to trial. The second justification concerned the nature
of his office. Rejecting all idea of divine ordinance, they argued that the
King was the servant of the state. 'The State at large is King', wrote a
pamphleteer in 1649, 'and the King so-called is but its steward or
highest officer.' Another writer declared that 'Kings are but the people's
creatures and the work of their hands.' Charles, on this showing, had
been guilty of a breach of trust 'against his dread sovereign the people'.

Man-made doctrines of this kind were cited by many, of whom John
Milton in his *Tenure of Kings and Magistrates* was the most eloquent.
But there were others who justified the attack on the King from the
Scriptures, citing principally a text from the Book of Numbers: 'The
land cannot be cleansed of the blood that is shed therein but by the
blood of him that shed it.'

Notwithstanding political theory and the Scriptures it was evident to
some of the leaders – most certainly to Cromwell – that the trial of the
King ought to be given some semblance of legality within the known
framework of English law. Although in the dust and heat of the conflict
he would speak of 'cutting off the King's head with the Crown on it', he
strove hard to perform this outrageous and revolutionary act as far as
possible in conformity with the legal procedure, if not the law, of the
land.

His opinions in the weeks before the trial are hard to trace with
certainty. But he had played no part in the forcible purging of Parliament
and it is at least arguable that had he reached London before (instead of
after) it took place, he might have attempted some less violent means
of excluding from the House of Commons those who opposed the trial of

the King, possibly by a vote of expulsion engineered from within. If this could have been done – and manipulations of the House of Commons almost as ingenious had been effected from time to time in the past – it would have looked very much better than the forcible overpowering of the Commons by military force which had actually taken place.

Cromwell after he reached London certainly worked hard to reconcile legal opinion to the trial of the King. He had several fruitless meetings with two of the most eminent lawyers in the country, Bulstrode Whitelocke and Thomas Widdrington, but failed to persuade them to countenance the proceedings with their presence and support. The same preoccupation with legal support is evident in the first draft of the Act for setting up the High Court: the two Chief Justices headed the list of those who were to compose it. They, together with all the other judges, made it clear that they would take no part in the proceedings. Their names were quietly dropped from the final version of the Act.

The composition of the High Court, as it finally appeared, seems to reveal a determined – if not very successful – effort to represent the different regions and the different interests of the nation. The members were carefully selected from almost every county, and they included landowners, merchants, lawyers, men with interests in overseas trade, industry and the American colonies.

Their names were published before the Court met, and at once the Royalists set up a cry of derision, declaring that they were all low-born squalid fellows, shoemakers, brewers and 'other mechanick persons'. It would have been a most interesting experiment in democracy if this had really been so. But of course it was not so. On the contrary, the names had clearly been selected with an eye to their respectability and social position. The list contained two peers (Lord Fairfax and Lord Mounson), two eldest sons of peers (Lord Grey and Lord Lisle), one Knight of the Bath, eleven baronets, and a number of substantial landowners. Among the merchant contingent there were two ex-Lord Mayors of London, and a number who had been Mayor of provincial cities. The Royalist jibe about low-born mechanick persons was based entirely on a small group of Army officers who were alleged to have risen from humble origins – an achievement which would today be thought entirely to their credit. They were Colonel Harrison, who had once been a lawyer's clerk, Colonel Hewson, who was called a shoemaker by the Cavaliers but seems to have been a manufacturer on a relatively large scale, Colonel Pride and Colonel Okey, who were said, again by the

Royalists, to have started life as brewer's draymen. It is on the whole more probable that they were white-collar workers – clerks employed by a brewer.

Membership of the High Court as far as the Army was concerned was confined to men of the rank of Colonel and above, and by far the greater number of the officers chosen were landed gentry. It was not, in the modern sense, at all a democratic tribunal. But it was, within the conventions of the age, a representative one since the members were chosen from different regions, different interests and, above a certain level, from different social groups.

Choosing members for a High Court of Justice was one thing; getting them to attend was quite another. Once again there was the contradiction between the grandiose pretension of calling the King to justice in the name of the people of England, and the awkward knowledge that very few of the people of England wanted to have anything to do with the business. A hundred and thirty-five members were named for this Court, but the quorum was fixed at the absurdly low figure of twenty. Furthermore, it was agreed that unanimity in the decisions of the Court was not required – a majority vote would suffice. This meant that, with a quorum of twenty, eleven votes would suffice to condemn the King. In the circumstances, the fact that never fewer than sixty-eight members actually appeared at the Trial, and that fifty-nine signed the death warrant must be accounted something of a triumph for Cromwell's organisation.

Was it all done by force? Eleven years later, after the Restoration of Charles II, in 1660, when the survivors of this Court were on trial for their lives, several of them told piteous tales of how they had been bullied and threatened, usually by Cromwell – who could not contradict them, because he was dead. Such stories are almost certainly exaggerated. Lucy Hutchison (whose husband, Colonel Hutchison, was one of the noblest of the regicides) sweeps them all aside. In her memoirs she wrote: 'It is certain that all men herein were left to their free liberty of acting, neither persuaded nor compelled; and as there were some nominated in the commission who never sat, and others who sat at first, but durst not hold on, so all the rest might have declined it . . . it is apparent they should have suffered nothing from so doing.'

It is certainly true that no harm whatever came to the forty-seven members appointed to the Court who never came at all, or to the eight who came to preliminary meetings but not to the Trial, or to the twenty-one who attended the Trial but did not sign the death warrant.

The weakness of the Court was on the legal side. A number of distinguished lawyers were appointed members of the Court, but few of them appeared. The best that could be done when a President had to be found to conduct the proceedings was to choose John Bradshaw, a barrister or modest distinction, who had had some experience as a judge in the Sheriff's Court in London, and had recently been appointed a judge in Wales. As an understudy for the Lord Chief Justice this was a weak choice.

Then, who was to prosecute the King? Here was another difficulty. The Attorney-General and the Solicitor-General, the Law Officers who would normally conduct a major prosecution for treason, had 'softly and silently vanished away'. Again a substitute had to be found, and the choice fell on a harsh eccentric from Gray's Inn, John Cook. He was a barrister of some ability and rather unusual opinions; as well as being a convinced Republican, he had written a book showing that free medical services, free legal aid and the strict control of the sale and consumption of alcoholic liquor were the essential foundations for a reformed Christian state. The best thing about him was his genuine, if rather dictatorial, interest in bettering the condition of the poor, and the worst thing about him was his vindictive hatred of the King and gloating pleasure in hounding him to his death.

For the King's death was, of course, the purpose of the trial. There was no intention of acquitting him. It was not to be a fair trial since its conclusion was certain in advance. But, if it was only to be a mock trial, what then was its purpose? Why not simply murder the King without more ado? The purpose was that of most *political* trials – namely to demonstrate the guilt of the accused to the world at large. Hence the King's trial had not only to be public, but very public indeed.

It was to take place in Westminster Hall, the great seat of justice for the whole Kingdom, and to be open to all. Moreover, it was to be fully reported. This is perhaps the most interesting and modern point of all. It was the first trial in history to have full Press coverage. Newspapers had come into being in England on the eve of the Civil War, in 1641. By 1649 there were no fewer than six licensed newspapers circulating in London, not to mention three unlicensed Royalist ones. We can rule these three out as witnesses; their editors disapproved so bitterly of the trial that they could not bring themselves to report it. But the six licensed papers reported it very fully. Two of them even issued supplements containing a verbatim record of the proceedings. The Royalists asserted that the accounts were incorrect and that much of what the

King had said was censored or omitted. But this does not seem to have been the case. The licensed reports contain so much that is extremely damaging to the Commonwealth cause, and set out what the King said at such length and with such eloquence that any suppression or serious misrepresentation of his words can be ruled out. The most favourable Royalist reporting (had it existed) could not have given the King a better showing. The only evidences of omission suggest a censorship of a different kind. The Party in power was anxious to suppress any evidence of fissures in its own ranks, and the various disturbances which occurred among the judges are omitted or flattened out. We know of them chiefly from the evidence given eleven years later at the trials of the Regicides in 1660.

The Trial opened on the afternoon of 20 January and there was trouble in the first five minutes. The Court, sixty-eight in number, had taken their places and the King had not yet been brought in. Lord Fairfax, the Commander-in-Chief, although he had been appointed a member of the Court, was conspicuously absent. When the roll-call was being read and members were answering to their names, at the name of Fairfax a masked lady in one of the spectators' galleries called out 'He has more wit than to be here.' Her identity does not seem to have been known at the time and it was assumed that she was a Royalist. She was in fact Lady Fairfax. The interruption was, however, only a matter of seconds. The Clerk continued with the roll-call, and as soon as he had finished, all interest was concentrated on the prisoner, who was now brought in.

Charles was dressed entirely in black and wore the ribbon and Star of the Order of the Garter. He was perfectly in command of himself. We know very exactly what he looked like from the painting by Edward Bower, who must have taken sketches in Court. He shows the King looking older than his forty-eight years. He was no longer the elegant monarch of Van Dyck. His hair was grey, his beard much longer, his cheeks fallen in. He looked haggard and tense but held himself regally. He carried in his hand a silver-headed cane, and presently, just before the reading of the charge, the head of his cane fell off and – as no one came forward – after a moment's hesitation he stooped to pick it up.

Now the charge was read by the prosecuting counsel, John Cook, with evident enjoyment. Charles, he said, had been 'trusted with a limited power to govern by and according to the laws of the land but not otherwise, but he had conceived a wicked design to erect and uphold in himself an unlimited and tyrannical power to rule according to his

will and to overthrow the rights and liberties of the people'. In pursuit
of this design he had 'traitorously and maliciously levied war against
the present Parliament and the people therein represented . . . and had
thus been responsible for all the death, destruction and disaster which
had been the result of these wars'. For this reason, 'for and on behalf of
the people of England', John Cook accused 'the said Charles Stuart of
being tyrant traitor and murderer and a public and implacable enemy to
the Commonwealth of England'.

During this diatribe the King betrayed no emotion, but calmly looked
along the lines of the assembled judges, and at one point turned right
round to take stock of the crowd behind him. When it came to the last
phrase – tyrant, traitor and murderer – 'he laughed as he sat in the face
of the Court'. President Bradshaw now requested him to answer the
charge. This was the usual request made to an accused man. He must
have been prepared for the King to question the authority of the Court,
because that would be the obvious thing for Charles to do. But he was
not prepared for the confidence with which Charles did it. It was
notorious that the King stammered; he had done so all his life. Now, in
his last ordeal, by one of those freaks of psychology he spoke without the
slightest hesitation. 'I would know by what power I am called hither',
he began with cold amazement. 'I would know by what authority, I
mean lawful' – he emphasised the word and threw in scornfully 'there are
many unlawful authorities in the world, thieves and robbers by the
highway . . .'. Having thus by implication compared the whole High
Court of Justice to a gang of robbers, he reminded them that he was
their lawful King. When Bradshaw tried to interrupt and again called
on him to answer the charge 'in the name of the people of England',
Charles remarked with great composure 'I do stand more for the liberty
of my people than any that come here to be my pretended judges'.

This was to be the theme of all that he said: namely that he would not
submit to a Court which had no justification by any existing law of
England; and that in denying the jurisdiction of this 'pretended' Court
of Justice he was protecting the true liberties of his people against an
illegal, arbitrary and usurped authority.

The first day was a bad defeat for the High Court of Justice, because
Bradshaw could think of no answer except rather stupidly to reiterate
'We are satisfied with our authority.' To which the King haughtily and
all too truly replied 'You have shewn no lawful authority to satisfy any
reasonable man.'

January 20 – that first day – was a Saturday. They had Sunday to think things over before the second session began on Monday afternoon, 22 January. This time they tried to startle Charles into answering the charge by telling him that if he refused to plead they would treat him as though he had pleaded guilty. Charles was not in the least put out of his course, but went straight on as before, asserting that, to defend the liberty of his people, he questioned the Court's jurisdiction 'for do you pretend what you will, I stand more for their liberties. For if power without law may make laws, may alter the fundamental laws of the kingdom, I do not know what subject he is in England, that can be sure of his life or anything that he calls his own.' It was a very shrewd blow. Only a few years before, in that very Hall, his minister Strafford had been arraigned for altering the fundamental laws of the kingdom by setting up an arbitrary jurisdiction. When the King now directed these same arguments against his accusers, he turned the tables on them in earnest.

Once again Bradshaw had not the experience or the authority to make an effective response. He merely said, several times over and quite ineffectively, that he could not allow the prisoner to dispute the authority of the Court. Charles for his part began to set forth his reasons for regarding the Court as illegal. This Bradshaw said he could not allow, but Charles persisted. 'Show me', he said, 'that Court where reason is not to be heard.' And Bradshaw, losing both his head and his temper, said 'We show it you here, the Commons of England' – which raised some laughter in Court.

By the end of the second day there had been nothing that could be called a trial at all. A prisoner who refuses to recognise the authority of a Court and will not answer the charge against him makes it impossible for any trial to go on. Why then did they not proceed straight away to sentence the King and cut the whole matter short? They were doing themselves only harm by having, in the end, no fewer than three sessions in which the King poured scorn on their authority and loudly asserted that he and not they stood for law and the people's liberties.

But they had a reason for making one more attempt, on 23 January, to compel him to answer the charge. The purpose of the trial had been to demonstrate his guilt before the world. Therefore they wanted very much to proceed with the trial in the normal way and to prove their case by calling thirty or forty witnesses in Court to tell of acts and works of violence committed by the King in person in the course of the war.

And so, unwisely, they let the farce go on for a third day and on Tuesday, 23 January once again Bradshaw exhorted the King 'to give your positive answer in plain English whether you be guilty or not guilty of these treasons laid to your charge'. But immediately the King started off again in a full flow of eloquence: 'For the charge I value it not a rush. It is the liberty of the people of England that I stand for. For me to acknowledge a new Court that I never heard of before, I that am your King, that should be an example to all the people of England for to uphold justice, to maintain the old laws, indeed I do not know how to do it.'

Once more it was the familiar pattern. Bradshaw tried in vain to regain the initiative, while the King smoothly and eloquently denied the jurisdiction of the Court and asserted that by so doing he was protecting the privileges of his people. Once only Bradshaw got in an answer: 'How far you have preserved the privileges of the people your actions have spoke it, but truly Sir men's intentions ought to be known by their actions; you have written your meaning in bloody characters throughout the whole kingdom.' None the less it would appear that by the end of the third day the general feeling in the public part of the Hall was becoming sympathetic to the King. The soldiers who guarded the Court were instructed to cry out for 'Justice', and indeed many of them may have done so quite spontaneously. But there were also noticeable shouts of 'God save the King' from the crowd, and even some cries of 'God bless you Sir' from the soldiers themselves.

As a demonstration of the King's guilt the trial was proving a failure. Public relations were not very carefully studied by the men of the seventeenth century, yet it is surprising that Cromwell and the resolute men who supported him made so little allowance for one of the best-known of all phenomena – the fact that a solitary prisoner bravely defending himself always wins a certain sympathy, and if he behaves with calm and dignity he is bound also to inspire respect.

According to the agreed schedule of proceedings, the High Court of Justice was to have sat again the next day, Wednesday 24 January, and to have sentenced the King to death on that day. But the trial had gone so badly wrong that the organisers had to change their plans. They had to do something drastic to alienate sympathy from the King and to remind the public that he had shed their blood in war.

So, desperately, on the evening of Tuesday, 23 January, they postponed the next session for three days, and announced that for the fuller satisfaction of their consciences, they would hear the witnesses against the King in a private session. This was not as good as calling them in open Court, but it did permit them to get their statements taken down

in writing and to give them to the press for publication. This meant that
before the King was sentenced to death, they would have placed on
record the evidence of those who had seen him in battle, and who had
heard him encouraging his men to kill his poor subjects. It was fairly
mild atrocity propaganda, yet the statements of the witnesses gave a
distinctly unpleasant picture of the King as an active and vindictive
leader of his troops against his people.

Strengthened by this, the Court met in Westminster Hall for the last
time on Saturday, 27 January to pronounce the death sentence on the
King. This proved to be the most difficult day of all. Early in the proceedings interruption from the spectators' galleries led to uproar.
Bradshaw in his opening speech reminded the Court that the King had
been charged with treason in the name of the people of England, where-
upon a woman's voice was heard to cry out 'Not half, not a quarter of the
people of England. Oliver Cromwell is a traitor.'

It was again Lady Fairfax, wife of the Commander-in-Chief. As
before, she was masked and does not seem to have been recognised.
Colonel Axtell, who was in charge of security in Westminster Hall, can
hardly have recognised her as the wife of his Commander-in-Chief,
because he ordered his musketeers to level their arms at the gallery
where she sat and sent a party of troops to seize her. Her companions in
the gallery were not at all anxious to be involved in trouble and, as one of
them said many years later, when the muzzles of the muskets were
presented so near the edge of their box, 'By this time we were very hush.'
In any case they prevailed on Lady Fairfax to leave, and when soldiers
appeared in the gallery to seize her, she had already gone.

The trouble of that day did not end there. The King changed his
tactics and very urgently asked the Court to adjourn so that he might lay
a proposition before Parliament. His request was eloquently put and
appeared reasonable: 'I do conjure you, as you love that which you
pretend (I hope it is real) the liberty of the subject and the peace of the
Kingdom that you will grant me this hearing before any sentence be
passed. . . . If I cannot get this liberty, I do here protest that so fair
shows of liberty and peace are pure shows and not otherwise, since you
will not hear your King.' What the King was going to propose can only
be conjectured. Possibly he was going to offer to abdicate in favour of his
son. Whatever it was, Bradshaw had no intention of hearing it. The
purpose of the High Court, in the minds of its dominant figures –
Cromwell, Ireton, Henry Marten, Ludlow and the Republicans
generally – was to destroy the King and the monarchy with him. It

would be a mere waste of time and a source of division to let him make any last-minute proposition.

But the King had spoken so urgently that he had sown seeds of division and before Bradshaw could formally reject his request another disturbance occurred. This time it was not among the spectators but among the members of the High Court itself. An insignificant member of the Court, John Downes, was so moved by the King's appeal that he began to fidget about, muttering such things as 'Have we hearts of stone? Are we men?' This was brave of him because he was sitting just behind Cromwell, who now faced round and said 'What ails thee man. Art thou mad? Canst thou not sit still and be quiet?' Poor Downes with a burst of hysterical courage said 'Sir, no, I cannot be quiet', struggled to his feet and, in what was probably a voice shrill with nervous excitement, declared that he was not satisfied.

In order to prevent disturbance Bradshaw hurriedly adjourned the Court. They all filed out to their meeting-place in the Painted Chamber and there, according to Downes, Cromwell turned and rent him. He called him a 'peevish troublesome fellow', and overruled his tremulous plea that they should at least hear the King's proposition. After half an hour or so, the members of the Court filed back into Westminster Hall intent on concluding the trial and sentencing the King to death, while poor Downes, as he tells us, crept away 'to ease his heart with tears' in the Speaker's room. (However, pity for Downes must be modified, because the silly weak creature came back to sign the King's death warrant a couple of days later.)

Meanwhile, in Westminster Hall, John Bradshaw addressed a final speech to the prisoner. In the lengthy, well-thought out and by no means unimpressive speech, he cited biblical and historical examples of Kings who had been called to judgement for their misdeeds; he emphasised the theory that the King was 'an officer of trust' for his people, and in a fine passage he described the mutual obligations of King and subjects:

There is a contract and a bargain made between the King and his people, and certainly the bond is reciprocal, for as you are the liege lord so they are liege subjects. . . . The one tie, the one bond, is the bond of protection that is due from the sovereign; the other is the bond of subjection that is due from the subject. Sir, if this bond be once broken, farewell sovereignty. . . . Whether you have been as by your office you ought to be a Protector of England, or the Destroyer

of England, let all England judge, or all the world that have looked
upon it.

This is the crux of the whole matter. Whatever theories may be
advanced as to the meaning of sovereignty on one side or the other – a
sacred trust from God or from the people – there was just one simple
practical point about Kings from medieval times to the seventeenth
century: their duty was to defend their subjects from attack and to
enable them to live in peace. A King who conducted the government in
such a way as to involve his country in a long and bloody civil war has
clearly failed in the primary purpose of kingship.

Now, at the eleventh hour, Charles himself seems to have felt that he
should not let his case go by default. 'I would desire only one word', he
said, 'before you give sentence, and that is that you would hear me
concerning those great imputations you have laid to my charge.'

Bradshaw overruled him: 'You disavow us as a Court, and therefore
for you to address yourself to us, not acknowledging us as a Court, it is
not to be permitted.' With that, the sentence was pronounced on
Charles Stuart as a tyrant, traitor, murderer and public enemy 'to be
put to death by the severing his head from his body'.

The King once more tried to speak. He did not apparently realise that
a man condemned to death is technically dead in law and therefore
cannot speak after sentence has been given. He was completely taken
aback when Bradshaw would not hear him and ordered the guards to
remove him. For the first time in his long ordeal his nerve showed signs
of breaking. He began to stammer. 'I may speak after the sentence' he
began and then stumbled on – 'by your favour, sir, I may speak after
the sentence. . . .' Then, in growing agitation because the guards were
closing in to take him away, 'By your favour hold. . . . The sentence sir,
I say, sir, I do . . .'. And then with the guards just about to remove him
by force, he made a wonderful recovery and spoke out clearly – 'I am not
suffered for to speak. Except what justice other people will have.'

He could not have made a more telling conclusion. The distressing
breakdown, followed by his recovery and this last parting shot were far
more effective than if he had made another of his long calm speeches.

The spectacle of a brave man fighting for his convictions against
impossible odds is always moving, whatever we may feel about his convictions. The dignity and pathos of his last three days has often been
recalled. He was to the end absolutely consistent. He reiterated on the
scaffold his unshaken views on his kingly duty and his belief that he had

sacrificed his life in trying to protect his people from arbitrary government by force. 'I desire the people's liberty as much as anybody . . . but
I must tell you their liberty consists in having . . . those laws by which
their life and their goods may be most their own. It is not for having a
share in government . . . that is nothing pertaining to them. A subject
and a sovereign are clean different things. . . . Sirs, it was for this that I
am now come here. If I would have given way to an arbitrary way, for
to have all laws changed according to the power of the sword I needed
not to have come here, and therefore I tell you I am the Martyr of the
People.'

He spoke with absolute sincerity; though knowing what we do of the
whole complex of reasons that had brought King Charles to the block,
we may not find his claim to be the people's martyr a very sound one.

Inevitably in any account of his trial the King appears in a more
sympathetic light than his accusers. He was one and they were many.
But politically, in the long run, the greater courage was theirs. Convinced, in the words of Cromwell, that God had witnessed against the
King and that he had deserved death, they chose to defy convention;
they did not engineer some hole-and-corner murder; they sought
(however unsuccessfully) to demonstrate the guilt of the monarch in the
traditional seat of English justice, in Westminster Hall, before a full
audience of his subjects, in a trial that was fully reported.

As one of their supporters proudly predicted a few days after the
King's death, their actions would 'live and remain upon record to the
perpetual honour of the English state, who took no dark and doubtful
way, no indirect by-course, but went in the open and plain path of
Justice, Reason, Law and Religion'.

John Milton, in yet more eloquent terms, praised the glory of the act,
'God has inspired the English to be the first of mankind who have not
hesitated to judge and condemn their King.'

The death of the King was intended to mark a beginning as well as an
end: an end to the Monarchy, a beginning of the free Commonwealth.
It achieved neither. The dominant party in the Army and their supporters in Parliament who had brought the King to justice were, for the
most part, men who saw little wrong with the social order in which they
lived, except only for the King's invasion of what they held to be the
rights of Parliament. They envisaged a Commonwealth which would
perpetuate Parliamentary government much as they knew it, but with an
elected Council of State instead of a King.

During the war a political party had grown up under the leadership of John Lilburne which asked for much more radical changes. The Levellers, as they were called, were a highly vocal and well-organised group with a fluctuating, but at times very considerable, following in the Army and among the Londoners. They demanded an extended franchise, a reformed Parliament and fundamental changes in the administration of the law. Earlier than any other group in the country – as early as 1646 – they had demanded that the King be brought to justice. But when the Army took control of events and the King's trial was planned, John Lilburne raised objections. He argued, quite rightly, that it would be dangerous to kill the King without first dissolving the old Parliament which had sat since 1640, and electing a new and more representative assembly. It was essential to create the basis of the new Commonwealth by passing the necessary reforms. Only when this was done would it be wise to bring the King to trial. If Charles should be tried and executed before a foundation for the reformed republican state was laid down, he predicted that the people would be no better off under the new government than they had been under the old.

He therefore drew up propositions for the consideration of Fairfax, Cromwell, Ireton and the principal officers of the Army. In a series of meetings between the Army leaders and the Levellers, on the eve of the King's trial, these propositions were lengthily talked out. It was palpably a delaying action on the part of the Army leaders, and Lilburne, incensed by their conduct, left London and withdrew from the scene of action throughout the trial of the King.

The mutiny of the Levellers in the Army which occurred a few months after the King's death, in May 1649, was the inevitable outcome of the rage and disappointment felt by this group because the execution of the King had had no effective consequences in altering methods of government or giving better representation to the people. The same unreformed and reduced Parliament continued to sit at Westminster.

The suppression of the Leveller mutiny in the spring of 1649 marked their extinction as a power in the politics of the nation. Later the convinced Republicans – whether their ideas were political like those of Edmund Ludlow, or fervidly religious like those of Thomas Harrison – were to be equally disappointed in the outcome of the King's trial. The setting up of a pseudo-monarchy, the Protectorate of Oliver Cromwell, was not what they had fought for.

The trial of Charles I was, at the time, an act of such outrageous daring as to startle contemporaries throughout Europe. Yet, though it remains the dramatic high point of the struggle between King and Parliament, its political significance was, in the long run, far less than was anticipated. It did not end the monarchy; it did not create a Republic. It was an incident far more remarkable in itself than in its consequences.

SHORT BIBLIOGRAPHY

By far the best text of the King's Trial is *A Perfect Narrative*, authorised by the censor in 1649 and reprinted several times during that year. It is reproduced in its entirety in *State Trials*, vol. iv. Additional material from the notes of John Phelps, the Clerk who minuted the meetings of the High Court of Justice, is included in John Nalson, *A True Copy of the Journal for the High Court of Justice for the Trial of Charles I*, published in 1684, but reproduced in its entirety in *State Trials*, vol. iv. J. C. Muddiman, *Trial of Charles I* (1928) follows Nalson for the text, but is marred by a Royalist prejudice even more extreme than Nalson's.

For the documentation, such as it is, of Cromwell's part in the trial, see W. C. Abbott, *Writings and Speeches of Oliver Cromwell*, vol. i (Cambridge, Mass., 1939). For the character of the press, see Joseph Frank, *Beginnings of the English Newspaper* (Cambridge, Mass., 1962).

For a general account of the Trial with discussion of the evidence see C. V. Wedgwood, *Trial of Charles I* (1964).

4. Oliver Cromwell and the Rule of the Saints

AUSTIN WOOLRYCH

REVOLUTIONS have a way of getting out of hand. Unless they are skilfully controlled by a close-knit, well-prepared power-group, they are apt to go far beyond the intentions of the men who first launch them. Few who assembled in the French Estates General in 1789 would have willed the Terror; millions of Russians who rejoiced at the downfall of Tsarist autocracy became appalled at the lengths to which the events of 1917 eventually led them.

In the England of 1640, most members of the Long Parliament were much more conservative in their aims than even the mildest revolutionaries of 1789 or 1917. They represented the greater landowners who traditionally ruled the county communities, and to a lesser extent the merchant oligarchies which ruled the major towns. They were members of a well-established governing class, whose interests they meant to reaffirm and strengthen. In so far as they had a social policy, it scarcely looked beyond the concerns of their own kind. Their prevailing political belief was in the sanctity of an ancient constitution which they imagined had existed from time immemorial; they came to reassert the fundamentals of that constitution against a Court and a government which, so they thought, had sought to pervert it.

In politics that meant the pruning of the royal prerogative and the securing of the rights of Parliament and the common law, which they carried through by statute during 1641. Over religion they were more divided, but most of them wanted no more than a moderate reformation within the traditional framework of episcopacy and a Book of Common Prayer. And religion, as Cromwell said, 'was not the thing at first contested for'; the majority of the politicians saw it as a secondary issue at the most.

Dr Manning has discussed the reasons why the moderate aims of 1640–1 led not to a settlement but to civil war. Most of the Parliament-men were profoundly unhappy about it, for civil war is a dangerous business for conservative men to engage in, and most of them knew it. Besides the slaughter, the destruction, the breaking of ties of kinship and neighbourhood and the awful drain of wealth, the gentry could not fight a war without arming their inferiors. And once thoughtful yeomen and husbandmen, craftsmen and artisans were called to risk their lives and livelihoods in battle, they were bound to ask what the struggle held for them. One of the most absorbing aspects of the English Revolution is the political awakening of large classes of men who had hitherto lain outside the political nation. They would not long be content to leave politics to men of birth and property to settle, or religion to their parish ministers.

Politics and religion were closely linked in the minds of these men 'of the middling sort', and their education in both proceeded apace during the war years. Congregations of Independents and sectaries sprang up in great numbers, and it is fruitless to argue whether radical religious attitudes were an expression of social and political frustration or whether the beliefs and practices of the sects themselves generated democratic political ideas. The interplay was continuous. The movement was widespread, but there were two special breeding-grounds of political and religious radicalism: the city of London and the cavalry of the New Model Army.

One reason why Cromwell's troopers fought superbly was that they believed they were fighting the Lord's battles. Many of their chaplains stood on the extreme left wing of puritanism, and instilled in them a faith that the overthrow of tyranny in church and state was only the first stage in the unfolding of God's great purpose for England. They saw themselves as the shock-troops of a second chosen people, and their goal was the New Jerusalem – the progressive realisation of the Kingdom of God on earth. They outraged the sober, orthodox Presbyterians with their demand for liberty of conscience, but their aspirations were not to be confined to the religious sphere. Richard Baxter went among them soon after the First Civil War and was shocked at the hold that the hotter sectaries had gained over them. Sometimes he heard them contend for 'church-democracy', sometimes for 'state-democracy'. The two concepts were easily linked in their minds. At one level the old order was identified with Babylon and they with the Israelites, the servants of an avenging Jehovah. At another, scarcely distinguished, King Charles figures as the heir of William the Conqueror and they as the victims of the Norman yoke. Baxter heard them ask 'What were the Lords of England but William the Conqueror's colonels? or the barons but his majors? or the knights but his captains?'[1]

This was the language of the Levellers, who found in the Norman yoke a potent historical myth. The Leveller movement first took shape in London in the immediate aftermath of the First Civil War. It drew its strength from those orders of urban society that the Great Rebellion had awakened to political consciousness but not to political rights: the smaller traders, the shopkeepers, the master craftsmen, the journeymen, and not least the apprentices – those distant forbears of modern student protest movements. It sought, less successfully, to extend its appeal to the smaller sort of countryfolk. To all who had suffered under the dominance of merchant capitalists or exploiting landlords the Levellers offered an ideology and a programme. Their demands are deservedly famous: biennial parliaments, a vast extension of the franchise, equal constituencies, radical reform of the law, popular election of magistrates, provision of free schools and hospitals, a code of indefeasible natural rights, and much else.

But a programme was of little avail so long as they were up against the implacable hostility of the Parliament and the city authorities. Their only hope was to capture the allegiance of the army and use it as an instrument of revolutionary action. Their Agreement of the People was mere paper without the backing of the sword.

About the Levellers' bid to win over the army and its ultimate failure I can say no more now; the story has often been told. The point I would stress here is that the Leveller programme was never the only expression that the aspirations of the politically underprivileged found during the ferment of the later sixteen-forties. When such men, whether soldiers or citizens or both, looked ahead and asked what the overthrow of tyranny should signify for such as them, there were always *two* strains in their hopes for the future.

The Leveller programme offered radical political remedies for their temporal grievances, whether political or social or economic. It held forth a kind of secular New Jerusalem. But there were always those who saw a more mystical and visionary significance in the victories with which the Lord had blessed the 'people of God'. The preachers of the sects and of the more extreme Independent congregations taught them that God was gathering His saints, that this was the beginning of those last times that the scriptural prophets had foretold, when the triumph of God's people would pave the way for Christ's kingdom on earth. For them, the unfolding of the millennium had begun.

For some years these two strains, the democratic and the millen-arian, were not in conflict. The Levellers demanded full religious liberty as a fundamental natural right; the sectaries raised their flocks on much

the same social soil as the Levellers, and felt the same urge to challenge
the political ascendancy of the great ones of this earth. The chief
Leveller leaders themselves had a sectarian background, and drew many
sectaries into their movement. There was always a latent inconsistency
between the Leveller ideal of equal political rights for all free men and
the more militant sectaries' feeling that only the godly should bear
rule in the New Jerusalem, but there was a way round this apparent
clash of principles. The Levellers, before circumstances forced
them to compromise, generally held that religion and civil government occupied quite distinct spheres and should be segregated, for
the civil magistrate ministered only to the outward man and should
have no power to impose on consciences or enforce any form of
national religion. That had been the view of that great sectary Roger
Williams. It was Milton's view too, and most of the sects went no
further.

But from about 1649 some ominous cracks began to appear. By that
time the Leveller movement was past its peak. Its rise and decline were
both rapid. Its first full-scale challenge developed during the upheavals
of 1647; its last serious bid for power failed when the Leveller mutinies
in the army were crushed in the spring of 1649. It was defeated because
Fairfax and Cromwell stood four-square with the Rump of the Long
Parliament in opposing it, and because the great majority of the soldiers
remained loyal to their old commanders.

But while this military defeat was the immediate cause of the
Levellers' failure, one reason why it proved so final was that the
Leveller programme was itself being called in question by people of the
same kind who had first supported it. Many of the smaller citizens of
London and some larger provincial towns, and many soldiers too, began
to ask whether a secular and democratic commonwealth *was* the kind of
dispensation that the Lord had in store for England. The contrary idea
of a rule of the saints was soon canvassed with increasing intensity. The
movement for a government by the godly in preparation for the
millennium began to gather strength just when the campaign for a
government by the people on the basis of equal natural rights was being
crushed in a one-sided trial by battle. It is as if the failure to remodel
politics and society on a secular, rational basis inclined many of these
russet-coated revolutionaries to look for a more apocalyptic kind of
triumph – to translate their hopes for a more just and equal society into
an anticipation of the cosmic drama foretold for the end of time in the
cloudy pages of the Book of Daniel and the Revelation of St John the

Divine. They read this heady stuff eagerly, with the literal minds of simple men.

Here by way of example are some propositions that a group of sectaries in Norfolk put to Fairfax and the General Council of the Army shortly after the execution of Charles I. They prayed the army not to 'be instrumental for the setting up of a mere natural and worldly government, like that of heathen Rome and Athens'. They asked

> Whether there is not a kingdom and dominion of the church, or of Christ and the Saints, to be expected upon earth? . . . Whether the kingdoms of the world and powers thereof, as kings, yea parliaments also, and magistrates . . . must not be put down, before this kingdom can be erected? . . .
> Whether this be not the time (or near upon it) of putting down that worldly government, and erecting this new kingdom? . . . How can the kingdom be the Saints' when the ungodly are electors, and elected to govern?

They proposed a government based not on the people as a whole but on the 'gathered churches', that is to say those congregations which had been voluntarily formed by a company of 'visible saints' coming together, testifying to each other of their experience of regeneration, and solemnly covenanting to walk together in the ways of the Lord. They envisaged a nation-wide federating of such churches and the election by them of general assemblies or 'church-parliaments'; 'and then shall God give them authority and rule over the nations and kingdoms of the world'.[2]

Now the whole history of Christian churches has been punctuated with episodes in which groups or sects have become obsessed with a conviction that the Last Times are imminent – that Christ is shortly coming again in glory, and that the Saints (meaning the faithful remnant that the Lord has saved against this day) must prepare for His reign by overturning all mere worldly principalities and powers. More than a century before the Civil War such beliefs had flared up among the continental anabaptists. Their violent seizure of power in Münster in 1534 had sent a profound shock through the European nations, catholic and protestant alike, and had intensified a bitter persecution. Tudor England had however been almost immune from Anabaptism; our Baptist churches stem from other and later sources.

Millenarianism entered very little into English protestant experience before the social and political ferment of the sixteen-forties created the right climate. But it caught on rapidly when the sober, orthodox divines of the central puritan tradition found themselves challenged by firebrand sectarian prophets who fed their humbler flocks with a wilder gospel. Not that the expectation of the kingdom of Christ was confined to tub-preachers and to soldiers possessed with the conviction that they fought a holy war. Some of the best-known divines preached to highly respectable audiences, including Parliament itself, that the struggle now afoot portended a working-out of God's purpose for the progressive establishment of His kingdom on earth, and that England was to be a second chosen nation. Cromwell among others was deeply imbued with the idea.

But it took on a cruder colour in some of the sects, and their millenarian note changed to a harsher tone after the execution of the king and the establishment of the Commonwealth. Like the Leveller movement, it was partly an expression of frustration at the small benefit that Parliament's victory had brought to the unprivileged orders of society. A group was emerging called the Fifth Monarchy men, and their temper was militant and aggressive. Their beliefs were a mishmash of Daniel and Revelation, with dashes of Zechariah and Ezekiel and Malachi; but the core of their creed was based on Daniel's dream of the four beasts. These were interpreted as the four monarchies or empires of the ancient world. The first three were variously identified, but the fourth and most terrible beast represented the Roman Empire. Rome however had not perished as Babylon and Persia and Macedon had perished, for its power had been usurped and perpetuated by the Papacy, and the Papacy was equated with the Beast in Revelation and with Antichrist. There was much fascinated speculation about the ten horns of the Great Beast, and particularly about the little horn that had the eyes of a man and a mouth that spoke, and made war upon the saints; this was commonly taken to signify Charles I, until the Fifth Monarchists came to cast Cromwell for the part. But their main belief, sustained by much fantastic arithmetic, was that the day foretold for the destruction of the Beast (i.e. Antichrist) was at hand. It was for them to fulfil the prophecy that 'the saints of the most High shall take the kingdom, and possess the kingdom for ever' (Daniel vii: 18), or alternatively that 'they lived and reigned with Christ a thousand years' (Revelation xx: 4). Their task was to 'overturn, overturn, overturn', in order to prepare the land for the Fifth Monarchy, the reign of Christ Himself.

There was nothing eccentric in the fact that men were searching the darker prophecies of the Old and New Testaments in an attempt to apply their meaning to their own revolutionary times. Virtually everyone accepted that the Scriptures were the revealed word of God, and a generation later Isaac Newton thought it worth much of his time to try and unravel their chronological riddles. What distinguished the Fifth Monarchy men was their emotional need to torture the cryptic figures in Revelation into forecasting a very imminent date for the millennium, and to read in them a divine call to violent action. This action moreover implied a social revolution, for the institutions that they were intent on overturning – parliament, the common law, the church establishment – were those that helped to sustain the political ascendancy of men of property. The cataclysmic irruption of an avenging God was to effect what the democratic programme of the Levellers had failed to secure, for the saints whose arms He would strengthen to take the kingdom and possess it were sure to be found among the despised and downtrodden of mankind.

Just how widespread the Fifth Monarchy movement became is more than we know, but it developed three main areas of strength. In London there were several congregations, but the chief was at Blackfriars, where Christopher Feake fulminated to massive gatherings. In Wales the itinerant preachers Vavasor Powell and Morgan Llwyd built up a formidable network of disciples. And thirdly there was the army.

During the early years of the Commonwealth most of the army was too busy fighting to take much part in politics. But when Ireland and Scotland were finally conquered, and when the battle of Worcester crowned its career of victory in 1651, the army soon showed the country that three more years of hardship and danger had only sharpened its revolutionary temper. A militant religious enthusiasm had taken a hold over considerable sections of the soldiery and not a few of their officers. These saints in arms found a redoubtable leader in Major-General Harrison, who was converted to Fifth Monarchist beliefs not long after Worcester.

For a God-intoxicated man, as in his fashion he was, Harrison was an unexpectedly flamboyant figure, with a taste for fine scarlet coats and gold hat-bands. But there was no mistaking his fierce sense of divine mission. Baxter describes him as 'of a sanguine complexion, naturally of such a vivacity, hilarity and alacrity as another man hath when he hath drunken a cup too much'. He had watched Harrison in action at the battle of Langport, and heard him at the moment of victory 'with a loud voice break into the praises of God with fluent expressions, as if he had been in rapture'.[3]

By the time that Harrison became an avowed Fifth Monarchist the army was becoming increasingly discontented with the rule of the Rump of the Long Parliament. During 1652 this remnant of a House of Commons elected a dozen years earlier was still resisting pressure to settle a more permanent constitution and make way for a more truly representative government. This is not the place to chronicle the army's various grievances, but behind them all was a feeling that these politicians were clinging to authority for the sake of the corrupt profits that power put in their grasp. The Rump, the army felt, was manifestly failing to measure up to what Cromwell called 'the interest of the people of God'.

A case in point was the Commission for the Propagation of the Gospel in Wales. This body had been set up in 1650, with Harrison at the head of its members, to evangelise the Welsh people, and through it Harrison had become the close associate of Vavasor Powell and other preachers of the Fifth Monarchy. But its term was for three years only, and when it expired at the end of March 1653 the Rump declined to renew it. Not unnaturally the House distrusted these millenarian firebrands and wanted to replace them with safer and more orthodox ministers. But Cromwell at this time stood close to Harrison and regarded the renewal of the Commission as a touchstone of the Rump's integrity. When it was refused, his attitude to the Parliament hardened appreciably.

So far, Cromwell had steadily resisted the army's pressure to dissolve the Rump by force. His veneration for Parliament as an institution was sincere, and he knew how hard it would be to establish a legally constituted government after such an act of violence. But as he complained to a confidant, 'he was pushed on by two parties to do that, the consideration of the issue whereof made his hair to stand on end.'[4]

The two parties were rival factions within the army. One was headed by John Lambert, the popular and able young major-general, and its discontents were mainly secular and practical. Lambert, as far as we know, wanted the army to set up a small Council of State to govern the country until it was settled enough to elect its own representatives once more. The other party was led by Harrison and consisted of the religious enthusiasts. Harrison believed that the time was now fully ripe for a rule of the saints, and he was said to favour the form that the Fifth Monarchist preachers Christopher Feake and John Rogers were urging: a sanhedrin of seventy godly men, after the model of Jerusalem's government in biblical times.

Although both parties were pressing Cromwell to expel the Rump he still held them back. In April 1653 the House got down at last to debating a Bill for a New Representative. But he found to his dismay that it proposed not a general election and a new Parliament but merely by-elections to the vacant seats. The Rumpers would sit on, and judge whether the new members fulfilled the qualifications that the Rumpers themselves imposed. Moreover there were strong rumours that they intended to remove Cromwell from the generalship and install someone more submissive – Fairfax, perhaps – in his place.

Cromwell now arranged urgent conferences between leading officers and Rumpers, and put to the latter one last expedient. Let them hand over authority to a select body of 'men fearing God, and of approved integrity', who would govern until the country could be trusted again to elect a properly constituted Parliament. Forty was about the number he had in mind. Clearly he was thinking in terms of a nominated assembly *before* he expelled the Rump. Late at night on 19 April he thought he had persuaded the leading members to consider this scheme before they went further. Next morning however they tried to rush their own bill through in his absence, and it was then that he summoned his famous file of musketeers and cleared the House.

It was a precipitate act, and he had laid no plans for what should follow. He set up a temporary Council of State, consisting at first of only ten men, with Lambert as its first president. But he referred the question of a more permanent settlement to the Council of Officers, a larger body whose membership fluctuated around thirty or forty. A military dictatorship was in his grasp, had he wanted it; but he did not.

Yet what were the alternatives? To summon a new Parliament by means of a general election, as the army had until recently urged the Rump to do, was almost out of the question. Not only had the army no shred of legal right to issue the writs, but the former members could convincingly invoke the act of 1641 whereby the Long Parliament might only be dissolved with its own consent. Moreover the army would have been bound to resort to arbitrary means in order to exclude its bitter opponents among the royalists, the Presbyterians and the Rumpers. It would have been a hopelessly risky venture, and Harrison's party would have opposed it strenuously on principle.

So it made a certain sense when the Council of Officers decided upon a nominated assembly as the new 'supreme authority'. It was to be a body of 'men fearing God and of approved integrity' such as Cromwell had lately urged upon the Rump, only larger and (within limits) more representative. The number decided upon was 140, with varying numbers of members for each English county and five or six apiece for Scotland, Ireland and Wales.

How were they chosen? The story accepted until recently, deriving mainly from Gardiner's *History of the Commonwealth and Protectorate*, was that the Council of Officers sent circular letters to the gathered churches in each county, inviting them to recommend such godly men as they thought fit for the trust of government, and that from the lists returned the officers selected most of the members. But Gardiner for once was wrong. There was almost certainly no general invitation to the churches, though some few churches sent in lists of names unbidden, and Harrison personally worked hand in glove with the Welsh saints in picking the members for north Wales. Only fifteen of the original 140 nominees, however, are known to have been proposed by their churches, and in fact the Council of Officers picked whom it pleased. Cromwell claimed later that 'not an officer of the degree of a captain but named more than he himself did'.[5]

The assembly thus summoned soon gained the nickname of Barebone's Parliament, because among its members was Praise-God Barbon or Barebone, the godly leather merchant and Baptist lay preacher of Fleet Street. But it was not called a Parliament by those who summoned it; it gave itself that title after it met. Some historians have seen it as a whole-hearted attempt to establish a rule of the saints, and assumed that Cromwell was converted for the time to Harrison's notions. This view needs to be qualified.

Cromwell never shared the crazier and more violent dreams of the Fifth Monarchy men. He certainly wanted a government that would promote 'the interest of the people of God', but, as his opening speech was to make clear, he regarded the assembly as an interim expedient. He set a term of sixteen months to its authority. He looked to it to bring the unsettled nation back to calm and prosperity, and to teach it the benefits of a Commonwealth so that as soon as possible the people could be trusted again to elect their own representatives. In his view and that of the more moderate officers, the task called for men whose puritan zeal was tempered by a sense of political realities, and where possible made respectable by birth and property. Harrison and his faction in the Council of Officers, which included men like Rich, Saunders, Mason, Packer, Wigan and Chillenden, saw things differently. They were not looking for a mere caretaker government to educate the people in the benefits and responsibilities of a self-governing republic. They wanted a sanhedrin of the saints, a dictatorship of the godly that would prepare for the millennium by overturning every vestige of the old 'carnal' government. It was they, we can be sure, who nominated the many obscure zealots who were to get Barebone's Parliament such a bad name.

Yet Cromwell evidently did not recognise the difference that lay between him and Harrison. He could be such a victim of rhetoric, his own as well as others', that he could not see where he was being led. He had his own vision of the Kingdom of Christ in England's green and pleasant land, though a less crude one than Harrison's. Early in June, just as the Council of Officers completed its work of selecting the forthcoming assembly's members, came news of a naval victory over the Dutch. Cromwell and the Council of State published a declaration calling for a day of thanksgiving. He hailed the victory – and surely the words are his own – as marking 'the day of (the Lord's) righteousness and faithfulness . . . of His beginning to heal the Creation; the day of gathering His people'. He saw it as 'an answer to the faith and prayer of God's people, and to their hopes and expectations from the Lord. It is a mercy minding us of, and sealing to us, all our former mercies. A mercy at such a time as this, to say no more; what mercies it hath in the bowels of it, time will declare: who knows?'[6]

How like this is to the speech he made a month later when he opened the new assembly and told its members

> Truly you are called by God to rule with Him, and for Him. And you are called to be faithful with the Saints, who have been somewhat instrumental to your call. . . . Jesus Christ is owned this day by your call; and you own Him by your willingness to appear for Him; and you manifest this, as far as poor creatures can, to be the day of the power of Christ. . . .
>
> And why should we be afraid to say or think, that this may be the door to usher in the things that God has promised; which have been prophesied of; which He has set the hearts of His people to wait for and expect?[7]

All too soon Cromwell was to be deeply disillusioned with this assembly. But before explaining why, we had better take a closer look at its composition. It was a widely variegated body, reflecting the diverse intentions of the officers who had chosen it. It was not for the most part the conventicle of simple, impractical enthusiasts that some textbooks still portray. Too much still lingers on of the royalist legend, typified by Clarendon's assertion that 'much the major part of them consisted of inferior persons, of no quality or name, artificers of the meanest trades, known only by their gifts in praying and preaching.'[8]

This is a travesty. No fewer than 115 members were justices of the peace – the very great majority, that is, of those who sat for the English counties or for Wales. Admittedly the office of J.P. had fallen in the social scale since pre-war days, but most county magistrates were still men of some substance, and so were most members of Barebone's Parliament. It boasted one rather moth-eaten peer in his own right, Lord Eure, besides Viscount Lisle, the heir of the Earl of Leicester. Four baronets and four knights answered Cromwell's summons, and a good two-thirds of the membership can be ranked among the landed gentry – though there were naturally many more of the lesser gentry than in a typical seventeenth-century Parliament. The company included Sir Anthony Ashley Cooper, the future Earl of Shaftsbury; Charles Howard, the future Earl of Carlisle; Edward Montagu, the future Earl of Sandwich; not to mention honest George Monck, the future Duke of Albermarle. Others such as Francis Lascelles, Richard Lucy, Sir Gilbert Pickering, Sir William Roberts, Walter Strickland, William Sydenham, Sir Charles Wolseley and many more would not have been out of place in a typical elected Parliament of that age.

Only a score or so had sat in Parliament before, but that is not surprising, considering that the great majority of former M.P.s, whether royalists, Presbyterians or Rumpers, were now so hostile to the army that they were virtually ruled out. But fifty-five of Barebone's fellow-members were to be elected to one or more subsequent Parliaments, mostly under the Protectorate; twenty-two would be called to Cromwell's new upper house in 1657; and twenty were to be back at Westminster under Charles II (fourteen in the Commons and six in the Lords). About a third of the members had been to a university, and despite the army's decision to exclude practising lawyers, about forty had studied at one or other of the Inns of Court. Thirteen of these had been called to the bar, so the House was not so devoid of legal experience as has sometimes been said.

One surprise is the paucity of army men in it. This is because Cromwell and the Council of Officers were so anxious to avoid any semblance of a military dictatorship that they decided not to nominate serving officers. The only exceptions were four of the representatives of Ireland, seven or eight governors of towns or garrisons, the two generals at sea (Blake and Monck), and five leading officers (including Cromwell and Lambert and Harrison) whom the House itself co-opted after it had met – though of these five only Desborough seems to have taken any appreciable part in its proceedings. It is true that about sixty members were called by military titles – some regularly, some not – but most of them had laid down their commissions long ago, or held rank only in the local militia. England had its own brand of Kentucky colonels in the sixteen-fifties.

We must now return to the central question of why this assembly disappointed Cromwell's hopes – and disappointed them so utterly that he was intensely relieved when it finally resigned its power back into his hands. The basic reason lay in a rift that very soon appeared between the more moderate members and the more radical ones. These are relative terms, for the moderates were themselves mostly reformers, as their legislation shows. But they were content to exercise the traditional function of a Parliament within the general framework of the law of the land. The hard core of the radical faction on the other hand was intent on proclaiming new heavens and a new earth, and on sweeping away everything that might hinder the imminent triumph of the saints. The split was not only religious and political; it was (as we shall see) social as well.

Was it Cromwell's fault that these divisions occurred? Professor Trevor-Roper has belaboured him for failing to provide the kind of leadership and management that might have kept this pseudo-Parliament on the rails. Of course it *was* naïve to assemble 140 men, mostly without parliamentary experience, and expect good laws and wise policies to flow from them by the inspiration of providence. Of course they needed a nucleus of well-briefed speakers and able tacticians to steer constructive measures through their rambling debates. Yet it is not easy to see where such a managerial core was to be found. It was certainly not found in the Council of State of thirty-one members that Cromwell left the House to elect as it pleased.

There was no unity even among Cromwell's closest associates, the men who shared with him the nominating of the assembly. Lambert and Harrison, each with a powerful following in the army, were not only at odds with each other; *both* turned against the new supreme authority that the Council of Officers had set up. Lambert withdrew from the Council of State from the day on which Barebone's Parliament first met, and he probably never took his seat in the House either. He retired first to his grand house at Wimbledon and then to his Yorkshire home. According to the French ambassador he resented the transference of power to the new assembly from the small interim Council of State in which he had held a dominant position. Harrison sat in the House and the Council of State for three weeks or so, but then withdrew in disgust with some of his radical friends. He returned only late in the assembly's brief life, and then probably sat only a few times. His motives were the opposite of Lambert's: he found that his fellow saints were not in command of the assembly as he had hoped, and that Cromwell's sympathies were falling more and more on the side of the moderate majority.

The rift between the two main groups in the House began to open in mid-July, after only ten days' sitting. The matter of debate was tithes, an old and bitter grievance of the sectaries. But whereas the moderates were prepared like Cromwell himself to consider some other mode of financial support for the parish clergy that would be fairer in incidence and less subject to religious scruples, the more radical members wanted to do away with any form of public maintenance and any kind of established parochial ministry. They wished religion to be left entirely to the gathered churches, each maintaining its own pastors by its own contributions, and all entirely independent of the state. This proved to be the rock on which Barebone's Parliament finally shipwrecked. An associated issue was the right of lay patrons to present to church livings. Naturally the radicals opposed it on principle, and they won one of their rare successes when they carried a vote to bring in a bill that would have abolished lay patronage outright.

The reform of the law was another bone of contention. Nearly all agreed that the law stood in need of considerable reform, but it was one thing to remedy the abuses of the common law while preserving its essential and venerable structure, and quite another to abrogate it lock, stock and barrel and to substitute a simple written code 'within the bigness of a pocket-book'. The radicals succeeded in setting up a committee to do just that. The Court of Chancery was a similar case. Something certainly needed to be done about its tangled mysteries and ruinously expensive delays, but to vote as the radicals did for its total abolition without erecting any other institution to take over its jurisdiction filled conservative men with dismay.

There are several things worth remarking about this persistent conflict between moderates and radicals. Firstly, these were not organised parties but loose groupings, whose strength fluctuated according to the matter under debate. Secondly, the moderates could nearly always command a majority when they turned up in strength. They did so early in November when the House elected a new Council of State, and they succeeded in turning nearly all the radical councillors out. But although one cannot give anything like firm figures for the strengths of these groupings, it is possible to identify a kernel of perhaps forty members who took the radical line on most issues. On some important ones they carried a varying number of fellow-travellers with them. And despite the withdrawal of Harrison and some of his friends they were mostly zealous in attendance, whereas the moderates were not. The House became very thin as the autumn wore on.

A further feature of this cleavage was the marked social distinction between the two main groups. Nearly all the men of birth and property whom I have mentioned were on the moderate side; the radical core was with a few exceptions of lower social status. These zealots were not for the most part the 'base mechanics' of royalist legend, but they included men who had been raised from obscurity by their careers in the civil wars, aldermen and the like of provincial towns, squireens on the shadowy fringes of the gentry, and a few others of still more modest origin. It did not endear them to the moderates that these pretenders to divine illumination were in so many cases godly tradesmen or Bible-thumping ex-colonels.

Cromwell was probably sensitive to this social factor when he complained in August that he was 'more troubled now with the fool, than before with the knave'.[9] He became particularly troubled because the radicals' aims implied an increasing threat to property. Tithes were a case in point, because so large a proportion of tithes had passed into the hands of lay impropriators and constituted a definite part of the value of the estates to which they were annexed. Advowsons, or the right to present to parish livings, were also a marketable property. The common law itself, which the radical threatened to destroy, was in large part the land law of the propertied classes. But what dismayed Cromwell most of all was the threat to do away with any kind of publicly supported parochial clergy. His main charge against Barebone's Parliament, years later, was that 'the ministry and propriety [i.e. property] were like to be destroyed'.[10]

The nucleus of avowed Fifth Monarchy men in the House was small. I cannot be sure of more than eleven members who confessed themselves as such, though these were just the centre of a larger group of radical sectaries who followed their lead. A little caucus of these enthusiasts met regularly to concert policy at the house of one of their number called Arthur Squibb, who was a thorough-paced Fifth Monarchist. They kept close contact, too, with the great prayer-

meetings at Blackfriars where Christopher Feake thundered the millen-
arian gospel.

This association with the most fanatical element among London's
citizenry brought the Parliament into increasing disrepute. It was a
nuisance to Cromwell in other ways, for the Fifth Monarchists were
doing their utmost to frustrate his efforts to make peace with the Dutch.
They were filled with crazy dreams of universal conquest. John Canne,
for instance, proclaimed as a message from the Lord that 'our proper
work is . . . not to look after merchants, as to grow great and rich by the
wealth of other nations, but to break their power and strength in
pieces. . . . Speaking here I say, as it were from heaven, that it is not
prizes, or the enemy's goods, our hearts or hands should desirously be
upon: But to destroy Babylon, stain the Glory of Kings and Kingdoms,
and lay low the high and great mountains of the earth.'[11] Feake's
congregation sang doggerel hymns of his own composing which breathed
fire and slaughter from the Lord against the proud and wealthy cities
of Holland. Harrison is said to have railed constantly against the peace
with the Dutch and against Cromwell for seeking it.

By the autumn Feake and his brethren at Blackfriars were denouncing
Cromwell himself as 'the man of sin, the old dragon and many other
scripture ill names'. The attack was extended to other chief officers of
the army. There was a proposal in Parliament that they should forgo a
year's pay. They were aspersed in the House as janissaries and denounced from the pulpit as pensioners of Babylon. Vavasor Powell 'told
the sword-men in general, that the Spirit of God was departed from
them; that heretofore they had been precious and excellent men, but
that their parks, and new houses, and gallant wives, had choked them
up'.[12]

Within the House the behaviour of the self-styled saints became
increasingly intolerable. They claimed to enjoy 'an extraordinary
call from Christ'.[13] They would come in from their religious exercises
with their Bibles in their hands and solemnly deliver their latest
promptings from the Almighty; one of them claimed for some ex-
travagant assertion 'that he spake it not, but the Lord in him'.
Moderate members heard themselves 'unsainted and condemned into
the fourth monarchy, and looked upon as obstructors of Reformation,
and no longer fit for the work'.[14] These zealots behaved as though
'actuated by a more high and active spirit of Dreams and Phantasie,
which set an end to reasoning, and led them out to a pretence of
infallibility in all their determinations'.[15] According to one report 'they

resolved to divide and separate themselves from the other members, who followed them not in their excesses, and to constitute themselves into a power distinct from them.'[16] They were said to be planning to remodel the army and place its command in other hands.

No wonder Cromwell looked on these proceedings with growing exasperation. No wonder Lambert quietly returned from his sulks in the north and began to work out a new written constitution that would set Cromwell at the head of the state, with a system of checks and balances to ensure there would be no more such excesses in the future. But Cromwell was not prepared to dissolve another Parliament by force, and he probably had no hand in the plot that brought this ill-starred assembly to an end. Lambert was probably deep in it, but the canker of internal dissension made the fruit ready to fall at a touch. The last and fatal conflict came over a scheme to settle the church and its ministry – a scheme long considered by a well-balanced committee and similar in principle to that which Cromwell was shortly to promulgate as Lord Protector. The first article was tensely debated for six days. When it came to a division the radicals mustered their fullest strength and probably exploited some complex cross-voting; at any rate the article was rejected by two votes.

That was on Saturday, 10 December. On Sunday the leading moderates caballed together and on Monday morning they came to the House unusually early. One after another they denounced their opponents for threatening the ministry of the church, antagonising the army, and jeopardising both property and the law. Then without taking a vote they trooped out of the House with the Speaker at their head, marched to Whitehall and resigned their authority into Cromwell's hands. A rump of about thirty radicals sat on until a pair of colonels arrived and civilly requested them to leave. Within a day or two a clear majority of the members had signed a brief instrument of abdication.

The rest is well known. Cromwell accepted the written constitution from the hands of Lambert and half a dozen fellow officers, and four days after Barebone's Parliament ceased to sit he was solemnly installed as Lord Protector.

It was not the end of the Fifth Monarchy men, though from now on they were an isolated and despised minority. Most of the sects accepted the wide liberty of conscience that the Protectorate extended to them. Harrison however broke with Cromwell completely, and on refusing to give any assurance that he would live peaceably was stripped of his commissions and briefly imprisoned. Feake and Rogers were also

incarcerated for a time. Cromwell did not want to persecute the Fifth
Monarchy men, but their open incitements to sedition forced him to
restrain them.

In February 1654 he summoned some of their leaders before the
Council to see what persuasion could do. There he and some Independent ministers argued at length with Harrison and Rich and two leaders
of the Fifth Monarchist caucus in Barebone's Parliament, John Carew
and Hugh Courtney. Secretary Thurloe reported their defiant views:

> That the present authority is not any authority, nor to be obeyed, and
> consequently arms may be taken up against it. That the magistrate
> which is carnal hath no right, nor can have; and the great objection
> which they make against this Government [the Protectoral constitu-
> tion] was because it had a Parliament in it, whereby power is
> derived from the people, whereas all power belongs to Christ. . . .
> Mr Carew added that my Lord Protector, when the little Parliament
> was dissolved, took the crown off from the head of Christ, and put it
> upon his own.[17]

The further activities and conspiracies of the Fifth Monarchists
cannot be chronicled here. They always looked back on Barebone's
Parliament as their great opportunity and their great defeat, and in 1659,
after Cromwell's death, some of them agitated afresh for a supreme
assembly elected by the gathered churches. Cromwell himself referred
in retrospect to his experiment as 'a story of my own weakness and
folly'. It provided one of the harshest lessons in his political education.
I do not agree with those historians who see in the Protectorate a simple
process of political reaction, but in so far as it marked a return to more
traditional modes of government Cromwell's experience of the militant
saints probably influenced him even more than his earlier contest with
the Levellers. And after the Restoration, when the royalists looked back
on all they hated most in the Great Rebellion, they were more apt to
remember the extravagances of the sectaries than the challenge of the
Levellers. Perhaps it was because the saints had come a shade nearer to
success; perhaps because the Fifth Monarchy movement was somewhat longer a-dying. It had its last fling in the cooper Thomas Venner's
crazy rising in 1661. At any rate enthusiasm was soon to become at least
as dirty a word as democracy. No doubt that was part of the climate of
European thought, but in England it was surely intensified by lingering
memories of the millenarians' brief attempt to set up a rule of the
saints.

SHORT BIBLIOGRAPHY

S. R. Gardiner, *History of the Commonwealth and Protectorate*, 3 vols (1894–1901) chs xxvi–xxviii.

Louise F. Brown, *The Political Activities of the Baptists and Fifth Monarchy Men in England During the Interregnum* (1911).

H. A. Glass, *The Barebone Parliament* (1899: at present the only monograph, but unreliable in many respects).

Austin Woolrych, 'The Calling of Barebone's Parliament', in *EHR* lxxx (1965).

Since this lecture was prepared for the press, Dr B. S. Capp of the University of Warwick has submitted his D.Phil. (Oxford) thesis on 'The Fifth Monarchy Movement'. This is now the best account of the Fifth Monarchists, and it is hoped that Dr Capp will shortly prepare it for publication. Professor Woolrych is writing a monograph on Barebone's Parliament.

NOTES

1. *Reliquiae Baxterianae*, Part I, § 73.
2. *Certain Quaeres Humbly Presented . . . By Many Christian People* (1649); extracts printed in A. S. P. Woodhouse, ed., *Puritanism and Liberty* (1951) pp. 241–7.
3. *Reliquiae Baxterianae*, Part I, §§ 78, 82.
4. Edmund Ludlow, *Memoirs*, ed. C. H. Firth, 2 vols (Oxford, 1894) i 346.
5. W. C. Abbott, *Writings and Speeches of Oliver Cromwell*, 4 vols (Cambridge, Mass., 1937–47) iv 418.
6. *A Declaration from the General and Council of State* (1653).
7. Abbott, op. cit., 63–4.
8. *History of the Rebellion*, v 282.
9. Boldeian Library, Clarendon MS. 46, f. 230.
10. Abbott, op. cit., 418.
11. J. Canne, *A Voice from the Temple to the Higher Powers* (1653) conclusion.
12. *Strena is Vavasoriensis* (1654) p. 19.
13. *An Answer to a Paper Entituled A True Narrative* (1654) p. 2.
14. Ibid., pp. 3, 9.
15. *A True State of the Case of the Commonwealth* (1654) p. 15.
16. Ibid., p. 20.
17. *The Clarke Papers*, ed. C. H. Firth (1891–1901) ii 244.

5. Swordsmen and Decimators – Cromwell's Major-Generals

IVAN ROOTS

'THE most intolerable experience England had ever had'[1] – this is the common opinion of the régime of the major-generals who, during 1655 and 1656, 'lorded it' over an England and Wales split into a dozen 'cantons'. Mercifully – some feel inevitably – brief, it is an episode that has still not been thoroughly explored.[2] Yet it is clearly of significance. Obviously it throws light on the many unique problems of the Protectorate. Oliver Cromwell had to clear away the lumber of civil wars and revolts and to thwart a would-be king who expected a welcome at home and gambled on backing from abroad. All this stirred questions, plots[3] and polemics, checking the drift towards healing and settling and calling for harsh exemplary treatment. This was something the major-generals might provide. But they could do more than this. They could help my Lord Protector with the day-to-day tasks that faced any seventeenth-century government, even the most legitimate. These amounted to getting something positive done at the centre and in the provinces, in spite of endemic shortfalls in funds, patchy information, cumbersome administrative institutions, unreliable personnel, tepid public-spiritedness and articulate, sometimes even fervent, centrifugalism.[4] Cromwell, of course, had one telling political argument his predecessors had lacked – a large, professional army – but this was not an unmixed blessing. Reaction to the major-generals showed that.

Something can be learned from comparing 'the personal government of Charles I' with the rule of the major-generals. The Eleven Years Tyranny of 1629–40 came after three heedless and rapidly dismissed parliaments:[5] so did the 'era of petty tyranny'[6] of 1655–6.[7] Both régimes levied heavy taxation of doubtful legality. Charles took tunnage and poundage without parliamentary consent, extended ship-money to the whole kingdom and contemplated an excise. Cromwell continued the excise actually brought in by the Long Parliament and raised heavy taxation, direct and indirect, by mere protectorial ordinance. Each ruler was involved in major legal disputes: Charles had his Hampden, Cromwell his Cony.[8] Both followed social policies in which high-mindedness was interlarded with mundane concern for public order. Each confronted religious dissidence running over into political animosity. King and Protector alike had to study matters of external defence and internal security and each dreamed of 'a perfect militia'.[9]

Looked at in this way, the rule of the major-generals takes on another dimension. Of course, Desborough, Kelsey and the rest were military commanders, but they were also parts of an administrative machine with ever-extending functions. In this they telescoped into a few months a process typical of Tudor developments which allowed to grow out of *ad hoc* commissions elaborate permanent institutions with broad responsibilities. Obvious examples are the Council of the North and the Court of High Commission. In a sense the major-generals combined the functions of each of these, busying themselves in both church and state. They were also like the French *intendants*, those agents of central authority introduced by Francis I and 'fixed' by Richelieu a century later. 'Intendant' was perhaps not a fierce term of abuse in England then, but to call a man 'satrap' and bashaw' was grossly insulting. These titles spoke of caprice and cruelty, yet they had an unintended accuracy. They stood for the permanent provincial governors of the Turkish Empire, an organised polity, much more sophisticated in reality than in popular imagination.

The major-generals came into the localities, then, not simply to bring in a military despotism or to lay about the enemies, actual or potential, of the republic, but to help fulfil the sensible intention of any ruler – a Philip II or a Great Elector – to govern, to get some effective central control, uniformity, commonly regarded as the antechamber to unity. Not that we can claim that the major-generals were set up deliberately as the first step to some fully worked-out system, one usurping for good the normal channels and traditional means of communication. But from the start a few possibilities were glimpsed, and before long the major-generals were seen as the main link between London and the provinces. They were showered with orders and instructions, just as the J.P.s – holders of an office which still survived – had been under the Tudors and the early Stuarts and as the county committees had been both during the civil war and since.[10] The result of all this was a monstrous apparition scaring the normal rulers of the countryside, who fancied they saw social as well as political and administrative revolution lurking in the dark shadows cast by musket and sword. The reflex reaction to this of 'men of substance' disturbed Cromwell's civilian advisers and supporters who were always nervous about his military associations and wanted to rescue him – and themselves – from the choking grip of the soldiery, grandees and rank-and-file alike. In the second protectorate parliament they thankfully threw the 'swordsmen and decimators' to the country members who hated them worse than they had ship-money sheriffs, committee-men, sequestrators and excise-men. The periphery triumphed over the centre once again.[11]

The occasion or excuse for a renewed effort in the localities had been provided by royalist conspiracy. Perhaps that sort of thing was always overdrawn, even when it could be linked with threats of foreign intervention. Its leaders were at sixes and sevens, its support confused and some of it demoralised, its planning and execution bungling.[12] Yet some day it might – it just might – pull something off. A lucky bullet lodged in the Protector's head, and the current order of things might 'be undone in an instant'.[13] Precautions must therefore be taken – more work for the sword. Yet all this must be 'a vast charge to the people',[14] a demonstration of unpopularity, a token of illegitimacy and an incitement to rejection. Somehow the vicious circle must be snapped. Cromwell knew all the arguments for easing the military burden, but how could it be done without lowering the barriers against intestine and external enemies?[15] This is where the appealing notion of a local militia came in. You could thin out the regular cadres, getting rid of awkward 'uncommandable' men, and form 'a new quickset hedge' of local volunteers, protected for a while by an old hedge of reliable professionals until the new one had taken root and grown substantial.[16] It should be cheaper. It might win the backing of men – of whom it was suspected there were many – who for peace and prosperity would be ready to accept a *de facto* government that was effective as well on the way to becoming *de jure*, smiled on by Providence.[17] They might stomach a new model militia better than the now old model professional army. At the same time there would be jobs for enough regulars to make it hard for them to complain of being pushed out into the cold. The new militia was in fact attractive to a wide range of outlooks – to the Protector, himself hankering after 'normalcy'; to John Lambert, advocate of a strong executive; to the civilian Cromwellians with the urge for retrenchment and conciliation;[18] to 'grandees' anxious for employment.[19]

There was a revolt in the south-west early in 1655, Penruddock's Rising, a gimcrack affair, soon put down.[20] It came so opportunely that many said it must be 'a trick of great Oliver's'[21] to justify new repressions under colour of the necessity of the times. To deal with it and its consequences John Desborough got a commission in March as 'major-general of the West'.[22] The emphasis here was on security, but already he was urged to work in with existent local authorities – sheriffs, J.P.s, county committees and a new body of commissioners – to establish, maintain and deploy a novel local militia. In May his area was extended. Meanwhile a few other special commissions had been issued, and there was some hectic activity in censorship, jury-packing and charter revision – all favouring more central control. Between August and October 1655 extension of the new militia was discussed and approved by the council of state.[23] On 10 October detailed instructions – later supplemented[24] – were given to named commanders for specified areas.[25] By the end of the month these were in print and the major-generals were travelling down to their commands.[26]

The instructions repay detailed study. The new district commanders were to 'prevent and break' the designs of enemies of the present state by 'suppressing al tumults' etc. Extraordinary powers for an extraordinary situation, Penruddock's rising being taken to be a foretaste of more serious things to come. But the same authorities are to give some of their time to searching out 'thieves, robbers and highwaymen' – a routine task familiar to more traditional officials. A strict eye is to be given to the 'conversation and carriage of all disaffected persons'. Horse-races, cock-fighting, bear-baitings, stage-plays are to be banned, not so much on moral grounds or because they give pleasure as because 'treason and rebellion is [sic] usually hatched and contrived against the state upon such occasions'. (There is an echo here of Laud's objection to 'chewing the quidd after lectures'.) The major-generals are also put to the poor laws 'in effectual execution' – shades of the Books of Orders of Charles I![27] Puritan zeal may be seen in the demand for promoting godliness and virtue among the laity and spiritual competence among the clergy and for regular reporting on progress in this field to Protector and council. Laud's visitations spring to mind. Bonds for good behaviour are to be taken from suspects, registers are to be kept of the movements of such people in and out of the country, within each area and between areas.[28] The motive here is, of course, security in the special circumstances of the time, but the appointment of a central registry,[29] like the registration of births, deaths and marriages proposed by the Nominated Assembly a couple of years before, suggests that there was some awareness of the uses of statistics in age which was beginning to create the science of political arithmetic. Other instructions – to investigate murders, affrays and other crimes, to license ale-houses,[30] suppress gaming-houses and brothels – show a desire on the part of the self-constituted protectorate to cope with the perennial problems of governments, legitimate or otherwise. The way in which different kinds of tasks were intermingled in the instructions suggests that the council itself was neither so willing nor so competent as the historian to disentangle the routine from the extraordinary.

The chief responsibility of the new-style lord-lieutenants at this stage was the militia itself, and the assessment and collection of 'a decimation tax' to maintain it.[31] This was a charge to be raised from 21 September 1655 of one-tenth on the estates of 'known' royalists of £100 p.a. in real property and £1,500 personal. The avowed object here was to prevent 'the whole kingdom [sic] being exposed to the rage and malice' of rebels actual and potential and to make these people pay for the machinery to keep them under control.[32] It meant treating them as 'an implacable generation of men'[33] – which some of them at least certainly were. But it might, unintentionally, make others 'desperate and irreconcilable', too.[34] In practice, it did persuade a few less than whole-hearted men formally to give up association with 'rash and inconsiderable persons' and to proclaim their willingness to accept the present government. Moreover, the levying of the tax must not be assumed to be capricious. There is evidence of the major-generals' desire to go about things in a regular, it might even be said, given their terms of reference, equitable way.[35] Some royalists tried to get out of paying by appeals 'at Court' or by pulling strings with local commissioners.[36] Some of them managed it, too, much to the chagrin of major-generals like Kelsey and Boteler, who found that even without this drain they were uncertain of raising adequate funds.[37] Many marked out to pay the charge became 'very industrious to bring their estates under £100 p.a.'[38] Sometimes they made it. Some major-generals complained bitterly about these evasions, arguing that the limits were set so high that some of 'the most desperate people escape'.[39] On the other hand, Whalley (Notts.) was opposed to lowering the level of incidence, because it might well alienate the 'middling' sort of men, among whom he thought, rightly or wrongly, support for the government was most likely to be found.[40]

If the major-generals differed about the imposition of the tax, they varied, too, in their diligence and competence in assessing and collecting it. The later instructions to send all proceeds to the army committee in London[41] suggests that they also had contrasting ideas on how to spend it. There was in fact nothing monolithic about these men. The districts over which they individually ruled were dissimilar in area, population, economic life, wealth and whatever else.[42] Berry had the whole of Wales and more;[43] Kelsey took over Kent and Surrey,[44] Skippon (from March 1656)[45] only London; Barkstead controlled Westminster and Middlesex. The principles of allocation are not clear, though overall wealth must have been one criterion. Yet wealthy areas might have fewer royalists to tax than, say Wales, where money was tight, but the proportion of royalists in the sparse population high. Much more investigation is called for here.

The decimators themselves shared high military ranks.[46] Otherwise like the royalists,[47] roundheads,[48] independents,[49] presbyterians,[50] engagers, levellers,[51] regicides, rumpers, members of Barebone's parliament, civilian Cromwellians or indeed any other group you care to name, they were a heterogeneous lot – in social origins, age, education, experience and so on.[52] They were not all nonentities – most had had 'somewhat to do in the world'. They came from various parts of the country, some, though not all, having a connection by birth or career with the areas assigned to them.[53] Several were kinsmen, if only by marriage, with Oliver Cromwell;[54] some had served with him in the field. But no easy generalisation can cover their relationship nor may any reliable conclusions be drawn from it. Kinship does not preclude bitter personal animosity. Experiences shared are not automatically unifying. Above all the major-generals parted company in their religious and political outlooks. This is most vividly brought out in the debates in the second protectorate parliament over the 'trial' of the Quaker, James Nayler. The major-generals took up diverse attitudes to the nature of his offence, to parliament's right to take notice of it, the sort of punishment it should have, and the implications of what was said and done in the Commons.[55] Lambert was remarkably tolerant, if not indifferent in religion, and eloquent on the bad precedents that were being established by parliament's headlong assault on personal liberty. Skippon and Boteler appear as ugly bigots, obsessed with sin, or at any rate anxious to give that impression.[56]

Variety of action and reaction may be traced among the local commissioners, too, though a thorough investigation of this has not yet been made. Certainly the lists of those nominated must not be taken at face-value. Like those for the county committees of the civil war,[57] they represent an angling for support as much as a confident expectation of it. Many of those named never served and were never likely to have done. Many nominees blandly ignored the summons;[58] others masked their

reluctance to turn up by offering feeble excuses – gout, toothache.[59]
This was predictable, of course; in fact, in Essex Haynes was frankly
taken aback at having such a good turn-out at his preliminary meetings.
His comment that there might have been even more there 'if some
extraordinary providence had not delivered them' has an ironic ring.[60]
The willingness of those who did serve must be looked at critically. By
taking office they might do something to mitigate the impact of the
central and military authorities on the local civilian community. Some
men persuaded themselves, perhaps, that if they themselves did not
serve, worse might. A letter of Thomas Crompton, one of the Staffordshire Commissioners, to 'his most worthy friend', Sir Richard Leveson,
and dated 18 December 1655, stresses how a sense of community among
the gentry could survive civil wars, regicide, Commonwealth and
Protectorate:

> I have received from his Highness and Council orders and instruc-
> tions for taking security of several persons of this county (amongst
> whom you are one) for their peaceable behaviour to his Highness and
> the good people of this Commonwealth; and also for their menial
> servants. Sir, the weather being very difficult and tedious for you to
> stir far from home, my respect I owe you commands me to wait on
> you either at your own house or tenant's house in Trentham, where
> you may be confident I will use you with what civility my commission
> and instructions give me leave, and upon my own account demon-
> strate my self
>
> Honoured Sir,
> Your most affectionate friend and servant. . . .[61]

Leveson and Crompton had both been 'neuters' just before and just
after the outbreak of civil war in 1642. Leveson had then turned royalist,
serving the king as an M.P. at the Oxford 'parliament' and as a garrison
officer at Nantwich. Crompton became a member of the Staffordshire
county committee and a 'recruiter' M.P. from 1647–53. Leveson was
worth about £1,500 p.a., Crompton about £400. For all their political
differences they were fellow-members of a community which still
respected gentility backed by property.[62]

No doubt some serving commissioners were genuine enthusiasts for
whatever cause it was they associated with the major-generals. Others
eagerly clambered on the band-wagon. Some were men who in normal
times could not have thrust themselves into office on the county level.
Many even of these were anxious to 'save themselves harmless' by

obtaining printed copies of their instructions and by demanding direct answers to pointed questions about things that did 'a little stick upon . . . them'.[63]

The attitudes taken up by individual major-generals towards sub-ordinates – sheriffs, J.P.s, 'old' committee-men, new commissioners, collectors and the rest – were variegated. Thomas Kelsey refused to be impressed by any of them and, it has been claimed, treated the county committee of Kent, an energetic and assertive one, as 'a cypher, a sort of local *parlement* existing merely to ratify his arbitrary decrees'. For all that, he had to push hard to get them to hand over vital records.[64] Some of his colleagues used more tact in winning co-operation.[65] They accepted that the experience of many officials, whose interests were commonly more administrative than political and whose careers were now at stake, made them 'fittest for this work'.[66] The 'seeming readiness' of others could be taken as a half-way stage towards genuine compliance. Certainly for many of the tasks to which the major-generals were committed expert assistance on the lower level was essential. In auditing accounts the pen is handier than the sword.

If some major-generals were optimistic in their relationships with older authorities, others could be gloomy – with reason. Worsley complained that he could 'hardly find a quorum of honest men' in Lichfield.[67] Boteler was certain that he should not trust any of the men named by Thurloe for his area.[68] Berry, saddled with the enormous and unsettled district of Wales, hovered between acute depression and mild hope.[69] Significantly, several major-generals wanted more J.P.s to be appointed – among whom they asked to be counted themselves.[70] On the face of it to become a J.P. was a trivial distinction for a 'grandee' – but the mere request suggests that the very largeness of their respon-sibilities gave the major-generals qualms.[71] The minor but more familiar office might help to regularise their position in the conservative eyes cast so coldly upon them. In fact these hard-bitten old soldiers could be very thin-skinned. Ludlow's sneer that they were persons 'who to say no worse had enlarged their consciences to an extraordinary size in the execution' of their orders simply will not do.[72] Their correspondence reveals a sense of isolation and an awareness of the awful burden of their commissions.[73] Some at least were uneasy. They had far more confidence in God than in themselves. Goffe's admission – 'I am weak' – in the circumstances sounds heart-felt.[74] Berry reported that a delinquent had appealed to him as if he were 'a little king that could redress every grievance.'[75] It was flattering, but it is clear that he did not consider himself endowed with sovereignty, divine or otherwise. The diffidence of many of his colleagues is apparent in the frequency and eagerness of their reports to Thurloe or to Oliver himself.[76] Besides setting out a mass of information about a miscellany of matters 'coming to [their] observation',[77] they show a yearning to be comforted with advice about the principles and detail of their assignments. They are pleased merely to get a letter from London – though they complain about heavy postal charges.[78] They are anxious to know how their colleagues are getting on.[79] In reporting their own doings they seem a little inclined to dwell more on what they are going to do than on what they have actually done.

Yet most of them were without doubt diligent and enterprising. Desborough had not a drop of lazy blood in him – he was in the saddle for hours on end, jogging over the rough roads, meeting, talking, deciding, and still getting off a couple of letters a day.[80] Berry did not let his dreams of a holiday stop him from getting on with the job in Wales, 'where men will rule if they be not ruled'.[81] Worsley wore himself out by thirty-four.[82] He died in June 1656 at St James's, where he and the other commanders had been summoned to give advice on major political and financial matters – an indication that the council still saw in them the makings of an effective governmental machine.[83] But hard work does not of itself guarantee efficiency. The standards reached by the major-generals varied according to the nature of their districts, their own temperaments, intelligence and so on. Again, faced with so much to do, different major-generals put different stress on different parts of their programmes. Kelsey was hot on decimations and the control of movements, reasonably enough, since Kent had from the start of the wars been strongly tainted with royalism and provided the shortest possible route between London and the Continent and back.[84] Whalley was keen on social and economic problems: wages and prices, weights and measures, enclosures, depopulations, the meetings of manorial courts – all these came under a bleak inquisitorial eye.[85] Worsley and Boteler, each in his own way, were dedicated to that moral and spiritual reformation that lay so near to the Lord Protector's own heart – and was so exasperating to meaner, more sensual men. Haynes and Berry took particular pride in gingering up J.P.s, mayors and corporations.[86]

Much, then, was intended; much but rather less was attempted; perhaps even less was done. Taking the major-generals as a whole, it is fair to say that hardly any part of their manifold responsibilities was utterly neglected. But equally no single major-general could hope to give equal weight to them all. The effect over the country generally was that everywhere some interest or other was upset, someone's toes were trodden on, somebody else's nose put out of joint. Conversely, some men, if only the inarticulate poor, may have seen something socially valuable, something they themselves wanted, in some parts of the major-generals' work. This aspect has not received the attention it may deserve. Yet the other things in the context of the sixteen-fifties and in the perspective of the whole seventeenth century were certainly more important. The energy and the potential of armed men from Whitehall made them the natural enemies of the natural rulers of the countryside. When elections were fought for the second protectorate parliament the swordsmen failed to fulfil their promises to determine its composition, though they did manage to thrust themselves on a few hapless constituencies.[87] At Westminster there was no friendliness for them among the country members and when 'the Court' and the Lord Protector abandoned them in their ill-timed bid for permanency, their 'system' collapsed, unlamented and unsung.

That fall is a whole story in itself, one complicated by personalities as much as policies. A main theme is that the major-generals in asking for the 'continuance of a tax upon some people'[88] showed that they would not or could not envisage an end to the emergencies which alone might justify 'sword-rule'. Traditionally 'good constables' were expected 'to keep the peace of the parish' without weapons and without too much on the rates. These armed men bore down too heavily – like Laud and Strafford, earlier exponents of 'thorough', they had to go. To have 'a little inspection upon the people'[89] was even more upsetting in the sixteen-fifties than in any other decade in the Stuart era.

There is much more to be learned about this expedient-cum-experiment. At present we have only vague answers to such questions as how much co-operation did the major-generals get? who gave it? why? who was indifferent to them? how efficient were they?[90] did they achieve anything positive and lasting? The truth must lie somewhere hidden in the tangled grass-roots of Stuart England and Wales:

> What, though the piping shepherd stock
> The plains with an unnum'red flock,
> This sithe of mine discovers wide
> More ground than all his sheep do hide.

With this the golden fleece I shear
Of all these closes ev'ry year,
And though in wooll more poor than they,
Yet I am richer far in hay.[91]

Like Death and Damon, historians should be mowers too.

SHORT BIBLIOGRAPHY

W. C. Abbott, *The Writings and Speeches of Oliver Cromwell*, 4 vols (Cambridge, Mass., 1937–47).

M. Ashley, *Cromwell's Generals*, (1954).

Sir James Berry and Stephen G. Lee, *A Cromwellian Major-General: The Career of Col James Berry* (1938).

W. H. Dawson, *Cromwell's Understudy* (John Lambert) (1938).

S. R. Gardiner, *History of the Commonwealth and Protectorate*, new ed., 4 vols (1903).

P. H. Hardacre, *The Royalists During the Puritan Revolution* (The Hague, 1956).

C. E. Lucas-Phillips, *Cromwell's Captains* (1938).

Ivan Roots, *The Great Rebellion 1642–60* (1966).

D. Underdown, *Royalist Conspiracy in England 1649–1660* (New Haven, Conn., 1960).

A. H. Woolrych, *Penruddock's Rising* (1955).

NOTES

1. John Buchan, *Oliver Cromwell* (1934) p. 459.

2. The fullest account is still the article by D. W. Rannie, 'Cromwell's Major-Generals' in *EHR* x. See also C. H. Firth, *The Last Years of the Protectorate* (1910, reprinted 1963, 2 vols); M. Ashley, *Cromwell's Generals* (1954) and Abbott, *Writings and Speeches of Oliver Cromwell*, iii and iv.

3. See particularly David Underdown, *Royalist Conspiracy in England 1649–1660* (New Haven, Conn., 1960).

4. Ivan Roots, *The Great Rebellion 1642–1660* (1966) offers the most recent account of the Protectorate and its problems. For government generally under the Stuarts, see *The English Revolution 1600–1660*, ed. E. W. Ives (1968), especially chapters i–iv by Austin Woolrych, Ivan Roots, Alan Everitt and D. H. Pennington.

5. 1625, 1626, 1628–9.

6. Buchan, *Cromwell*, p. 459.

7. The Long Parliament, dissolved April 1653; the Nominated Assembly, 'resigned' December 1653; and the first protectorate parliament, dissolved January 1655. Cromwell's relations with his parliaments are discussed by H. R. Trevor-Roper in *Religion, the Reformation and Social Change* (1967) ch. 7.

8. Abbott, *Writings*, iii pp. 498–9.

9. For Charles I and the militia, see Boynton, *The Elizabethan Militia* (1967) and T. G. Barnes, *Somerset 1625–1640* (1961).

10. For the county committees, see A. M. Everitt, *The Community of Kent*

and the Great Rebellion (Leicester, 1966); A. M. Everitt, *Suffolk and the Great Rebellion* (Suffolk Records Society, 1960); D. H. Pennington and I. A. Roots, *The Committee at Stafford 1643–45* (Manchester, 1957); D. H. Pennington, 'The County Community at War' in *The English Revolution*, ed. Ives; and L. Glow, 'House of Commons Committees and County Committees 1640–1644' (unpublished Ph.D. thesis, University of Adelaide, 1963).

11. Ludlow reports a Berkshire farmer complaining that he knew what to say to local men, 'but these swordsmen are too strong for me'. (Edmund Ludlow, *Memoirs*, ii 3.) Ironically, it is also possible to see the régime of the major-generals as a response to demands for attention to provincial interests. During the Interregnum there were petitions for the revival of something like the Council of the North. It was claimed that 'many necessary things are not presented by reason of the tediousness and great expense of . . . journeys' to London. John Lambert was in favour of decentralising the law courts and of establishing a northern university. See also *TSP* iii 324, where setting up a Sussex militia is recommended to obviate the need to send '*as far as London* for orders'. (My italics.)

12. See Underdown, *Royalist Conspiracy*, and A. H. Woolrych, *Penruddock's Rising* (1955).

13. *TSP* iii 122.

14. *TSP* iii.

15. *TSP* iii 319 refers to cavaliers who 'thinke to escape by favour, and may remayne as nest-eggs, to cherish others, hereafter, that may prove a pest to his highnesse and the commonwealth'.

16. *TSP* iii 160.

17. For a stimulating study of 'loyalism' – the positive acceptance of the 'powers that be' rather than those 'that ought to be' as saviours of society – see J. M. Wallace, *Destiny His Choice* (Cambridge, 1968).

18. The French ambassador claimed that the precipitate dissolution of parliament in January 1655 had no other motive 'than the reduction of the army': *TSP* iii 122.

19. The 'ill-condition' of the army should also be taken into account. See e.g. *TSP* iii 247.

20. The best account is in Woolrych, *Penruddock's Rising*.

21. *TSP* iii 122.

22. Abbott, *Writings*, iii 794.

23. Abbott, *Writings*, iii 644, 661, 666.

24. See e.g. *TSP* iv 341.

25. *The Parliamentary or Constitutional History of England*, 24 vols (1751–62) iv 461–7.

26. *TSP* iv 107, 116–17.

27. See E. M. Leonard, *The Early History of English Poor Relief* (Cambridge, 1900, reprinted 1965).

28. BM Add. *MSS* 19516, 34011–17 contain registry papers. Material on Surrey is printed and commented upon in *Surrey Archaeological Collections*, xiv 164–80.

29. It was not a strikingly efficient institution. Some of its agents were slack, incompetent, even stupid. Their writing was sometimes illegible, they muddled names and addresses, they failed to render complete returns and gave inadequate instructions to travellers. The officer at Dover sent some reports to his chief in London to 'a place utterly unknown'.

30. The problem of 'superfluous ale-houses' was a perennial and, in the conditions of the seventeenth century, probably an insoluble one. Ale-houses meant drinking, drinking loosened tongues an dencouraged a reduction in standards of

D

conduct which contributed to difficulties in establishing and maintaining public order. Moreover, the multiplicity of ale-houses, by diverting grain, chiefly barley, from food-supply, intensified social discontents. The question of stability lies at the heart of moral, social and economic policies during this period.

31. Roots, *The Great Rebellion*, p. 195.

32. *TSP* iv 132–3, 'This additional strength must draw with it an additional charge. Who must bear this? Must the well-affected? What so just as to put the charge upon those who are the occasion of it? This is the ground of the decimation.' See also *TSP* iii 282, 385. The government, of course, recognised that 'some other people' than the royalists were a threat to security, e.g. fifth monarchists and leveller terrorists. See Cromwell's speech of 17 September 1656 in Abbott, *Writings*, iv 260–79.

33. *TSP* iv 225.

34. Ludlow, *Memoirs*, i 405.

35. *TSP* iv and v *passim*. Major-General Haynes, perhaps correctly, regarded the decimation as 'the most difficult part' of his assignment: *TSP* iv 170–1. PRO SP 28 (The Commonwealth Exchequer Papers) contain a mass of material on the decimation, as on other aspects of the work of the major-generals.

36. E.g. *TSP* iv 241, 293, 364–6; Everitt, *Community of Kent*, p. 292; Abbott, *Writings*, iv 190.

37. *TSP* iv 224, 234.

38. E.g., *TSP* iv 344. Col. Bullen Reymes claimed that of his estate of £140 p.a., two-thirds was mortgaged for repayment of debts. Even so, his tax was fixed at £14 13s 4d: H. F. Kaufman, *Conscientious Cavalier* (1962) pp. 173–4. Some royalists evaded or reduced the tax by putting part of their estates in the hands of trustees.

39. E.g., *TSP* iv 218, 234, 316, 320. 321, 333, 336–7.

40. *TSP* iv 308. Goffe thought that 'the stress of this business [i.e. the work of the local commissioners] must be upon the middle sort of men': *TSP* iv 160.

41. *TSP* iv 297–8. *Cal. S.P. Dom. 1655–6*, pp. 140, 367–8; Abbott, *Writings*, iii 190.

42. Kent and Surrey (Thomas Kelsey); Sussex, Hants, Berks (William Goffe); Glos., Wilts., Dorset, Somerset, Devon, Cornwall (John Desborough); Warwicks., Lincs., Notts., Derbys., Leics. (Edward Whalley); Oxon., Bucks., Herts., Cambs., Isle of Ely, Essex, Norfolk, Suffolk (Charles Fleetwood); Northants., Beds., Rutland, Huntingdon (William Boteler); Hereford, Salop, Worcs., N. and S. Wales (James Berry); Cheshire, Lancs., Staffs. (Charles Worsely); Yorks., Co. Durham, Cumberland, Westmorland, Northumberland (John Lambert); Middx and Westminster (John Barkstead); London (Phillip Skippon).

43. For Berry, see Sir James Berry and S. G. Lee, *A Cromwellian Major-General* (Oxford, 1938).

44. Kelsey's activities in Kent are summarised by A. M. Everitt in *The Community of Kent*, ch. viii.

45. Skippon was appointed after a personal approach to the City by the Protector.

46. They did not in fact all hold rank as major-generals. Note that Lambert was represented by deputies, Cols Robert Lilburne and Charles Howard. Fleetwood's deputy was Col Hezekiah Haynes.

47. See P. H. Hardacre, *The Royalists during the Puritan Revolution* (The Hague, 1956) and Underdown, *Royalist Conspiracy*.

48. Diversity among parliamentary (and royalist) M.P.s is established by D. Brunton and D. H. Pennington, *Members of the Long Parliament* (1953,

reprinted 1968) and M. F. Keeler, *The Long Parliament* (Philadelphia, 1954). See also Hexter, *The Reign of King Pym*; V. Pearl, 'Oliver St John and the Middle Group in the Long Parliament', *EHR* lxxi, and the thesis by L. Glow referred to in note 10 above; V. Pearl, 'The "Royal Independents" in the English Civil War', *TRHS*, 5 Ser., xviii.

49. G. Yule, *The Independents in the English Civil War* (Cambridge, 1958); D. Underdown, 'The Independents Reconsidered', *JBS* iii, and G. Yule, 'Independents and Revolutionaries', ibid., vii.

50. J. H. Hexter, 'The Problem of the Presbyterian Independents', in his *Reappraisals in History* (1961).

51. 'We were an heterogenial body consisting of parts very diverse from one another, settled upon principles inconsistent one with another': Henry Denne, *The Levellers Designe Discovered* (1649) p. 8, quoted in 'The Levellers and Democracy' by J. G. Davis, *PP* no. 40.

52. See Ashley, *Cromwell's Generals, passim*. Some of the major-generals appear in *The Dictionary of National Biography*. Lambert was a gentleman, a grazier with a university education. Boteler was educated at Oundle. Desborough's accent was rustic – like Cromwell's – but he was a qualified attorney. The status of Lilburne was much stressed by Col Robert's brother, 'free-born John' the Leveller. Barkstead was a goldsmith's son. Kelsey was reputed to be a button-maker. Berry came from an industrial family in the West Midlands. Skippon was a professional soldier risen from the ranks. Mrs Hutchinson's blanket description of the major-generals as 'silly mean fellows' seems unjust. A comparison with the members of the Nominated Assembly – also often lightly dismissed as nonentities – is instructive.

53. Kelsey had been governor of Dover Castle. Skippon was commander of the London militia at Turnham Green in 1642. Barkstead was lieutenant of the Tower of London. Whalley had Nottinghamshire kin.

54. Whalley was the Protector's cousin, Fleetwood his son-in-law and Desborough his brother-in-law. Goffe was Whalley's son-in-law. Lambert was commonly regarded as 'Cromwell's understudy'.

55. See Roots, *The Great Rebellion*, ch. xxii, and T. A. Wilson and F. J. Merli, 'Naylor's Case and the Dilemma of the Protectorate', *University of Birmingham Historical Journal*, x.

56. See the debates as recorded in *The Parliamentary Diary of Thomas Burton*, ed. T. Rutt, 4 vols (1828).

57. See the references in note 10 above.

58. *TSP* iii–iv, *passim*.

59. *TSP* iv 391.

60. *TSP* iv 320.

61. Staffs. Record Office, D. 593 (Leveson Correspondence). I owe this reference to Mr J. T. Pickles.

62. Pennington and Roots, *Committee at Stafford*, p. 351.

63. *TSP* iv 211, 300, 301, 302.

64. Everitt, *Community of Kent*, p. 292; SP 28/234.

65. *TSP* iv 272.

66. *TSP* iv 229.

67. *TSP* iv 224. See also *TSP* iv 300 for a comment on the commissioners for ejecting scandalous ministers.

68. *TSP* iv 197.

69. See e.g. *TSP* iv 334–5, and Berry and Lee, *Cromwellian Major-General*, *passim*.

70. *TSP* v 353; *Cal. S. P. Dom. 1656–7* pp. 87–8.

71. *TSP* iv 197, 240–1, 316, 353, 393–4.

72. Ludlow, *Memoirs*, ii 20.

73. See e.g. *TSP* iv 359–60; *Cal. S. P. Dom. 1656–7*, pp. 87–8. Goffe reported to Thurloe that some Sussex J.P.s were troubled not to have a *custos rotulorum*, 'some of them saying that deficit may make all their proceedings questionable': *TSP* iv 394.

74. *TSP* iv 151.

75. *TSP* iv 237.

76. *TSP* iv and v *passim*.

77. *TSP* iv 277.

78. See e.g. *TSP* iv 217, 322. Several of the major-generals at the end of their service claimed to be out of pocket on these and other charges.

79. See e.g. *TSP* iv 233, 292, 308.

80. *TSP* iv 391.

81. Berry and Lee, *Cromwellian Major-General*, p. 180; *TSP* iv 292. Like Edward I, Berry was an advocate of overawing Wales by 'here and there a castle'.

82. *TSP* iv 179, 247–8, 340–1. Worsley constantly saw 'the finger of God going along with' his work: *TSP* iv 149, 187. Whalley was another very conscientious worker. See e.g. *TSP* iv 156, 185.

83. They were in London some weeks, returning to their districts on 17 June 1656.

84. See Everitt, *Community of Kent, passim.* PRO SP 28/159; SP 28/234. BM Add. MSS 34013–14.

85. See e.g. *TSP* iv 533–4, 685–7, 211–12.

86. *TSP* iv 320, 330, 396.

87. See e.g. *TSP* v 308, 341; Everitt, *Community of Kent*, pp. 296–7; *Calendar of Wynn (of Gwyndir) Papers* (Aberystwyth, 1926) pp. 345–6; Rannie, 'Cromwell's Major-Generals', *EHR* x 499–500; Roots, *The Great Rebellion*, pp. 197–8.

88. Burton, *Parliamentary Diary*, i 230. A receipt dated 26 March 1657 in PRO SP 28/234 refers to 'the Decimators ending at Christmas last'. See also Ludlow, *Memoirs*, ii 19–20.

89. Abbott, *Writings*, iv 269 (speech of 17 September 1656).

90. I believe that they were by no means as efficient as might be supposed from the strictures of their enemies who, 'mightly enraged' by the whole affair (*TSP* iv 176–7), described everything they did in alarmist terms.

91. Andrew Marvell, 'Damon the Mower'.

6. The Civil War and the Class Struggle

ROBERT ASHTON

HAVING nothing to lose but their reputations, English historians of our seventeenth-century revolutions do not run the same occupational risks as their French colleagues, who on more than one occasion have hazarded life and limb in publicly offering new interpretations of the French Revolution. For reasons which are not related solely to the different proximity of these events in time to our own day, the Great Rebellion has not bitten so deeply into the national consciousness of England as has the French Revolution into that of France. Certainly the historical succession of Monarchy, Republic and Empire which marks the course of French history between 1789 and 1871 and which continued to exert a baleful effect upon the political life of the Third Republic for a long time afterwards has had no counterpart in recent English history. The Gloucestershire yokel who once dismissed the late Professor Tawney's inquiry into the reasons why the inhabitants of his village always voted solidly Labour, and those of one of its neighbours equally solidly Conservative, with the startling observation that this was because 'they were for the King and we were for the Parliament', may have believed what he said, but his thesis could hardly be regarded as providing a useful insight into modern electoral behaviour. Indeed, if the average Englishman's politics are influenced in the least by his view of history, this is more often than not a view which ignores, or at least plays down, the passions and animosities which produced the struggles of the 1640s. He is nurtured on a few platitudes about freedom broadening down from precedent to precedent, which flatter his belief that things in England are ordered differently and that the events of the middle of the seventeenth century are a somewhat distasteful, untypical and un-English episode which is perhaps best forgotten. One of the most eminent of contemporary English historians of the seventeenth century has, in fact, suggested that the Civil War and Interregnum are no more than 'an untidy interruption' in the normal flow of English

history, which resumed in 1660 from where it had left off before 1640 –
not even before 1641.[1]

In taking this view Professor Trevor-Roper was reacting against
recent interpretations of the causes and consequences of the English
Civil War, which have been at pains to emphasise firstly, that the war
was the necessary outcome of a situation in which the further progress
of Capitalism had become impossible without the overthrow of a
régime which cramped and stifled it at every turn, and secondly, that
the monarchy which was restored in 1660 was a very different institution,
in terms of its administrative machinery, its financial dependence and
its economic and colonial policies, from that which had been over-
thrown in 1649. The greater part of this paper is concerned with some of
the problems arising out of the first of these considerations, and, more
particularly, with the relationship between ideologies and economic
interests in the struggles of the early seventeenth century. On the second,
I will confine myself to the observation that it is difficult to see in the
government of Restoration England an executive instrument of the rule
of the *bourgeoisie*.

There is however, another, far simpler and more fundamental reason
why 1649 marks a watershed in English history, and this is that to cut
off the head of one's king is, to say the least, a very positive and quite
irremediable act. Of course, in the Middle Ages kings had occasionally
been done to death in dark and secret places, but never with the publicity
nor the claim of legality which characterised the condemnation and
execution of Charles I. This was the great climacteric event which,
above all else, explains the changed character of post-Restoration
politics. This was the sacrifice for which no atonement could be too
great, in face of the recognition of which fact passive obedience was the
only viable and honourable political attitude. As Macaulay pointed out
long ago, High Tory squires might complain of the expenses of a lavish
court and of the ingratitude shown by their royal master to those who
had suffered for their beliefs during the long Cromwellian night, but
they were the first to rush to his defence whenever his God-given
authority appeared to be challenged by the forces of political and religious
dissent, which, in turn, were now inevitably tarred with a republican
brush. For all the effusions of a Sibthorpe or a Mainwaring, the classical
period of high non-resistance Cavalier Toryism is, in fact, not the early
Stuart but the post-Restoration period, and, most of all, the years of the
Exclusion Crisis and its aftermath. It was then that Sir Robert Filmer's
treatise, which had lain obscurely for forty years in manuscript, was

published and its message eagerly devoured by Tory parsons and even squires – many of whom, despite Macaulay's celebrated caricature, could read without undue difficulty – for it had now acquired a new poignancy and emotive power as a consequence of the unforgivable parricide of 1649. And so it was that later Stuart England came to accept what early Stuart England would never have accepted, the accession of a Catholic king. And the next revolution was an event of a quite different order from its predecessor; truly 'glorious' in the ingenuity of its compromise. The House of Orange had no greater liking for Republicanism than had that of Stuart. Indeed, it had far too much experience of it, although in the Netherlands the martyrs had all been on the anti-monarchical side. So, with the aid of a fictitious abdication and a fictitious warming-pan, the miracle was achieved whereby the monarchical and hereditary principle was preserved for all but the tenderest of passively obedient consciences, while English freedom was able to broaden down still further without any sacrifice of the profound psychological advantages of monarchical institutions. England gained on both the roundabouts and the swings.

It is one of the less dreary truisms of historiography that each age interprets the past in the light of its own experience. Notwithstanding the mood of doubt which afflicted many of the most sensitive Victorians, the hegemony of Great Britain was a basic fact of the life of mid-Victorian England. Representative institutions, England's greatest political gift to humanity, had long ago triumphed at home, and, linked somewhat optimistically with the growth of national consciousness on the continent, bade fair to spread themselves over the face of much of contemporary Europe. In these circumstances it is hardly surprising that contemporary historians were inclined to see in the development of these institutions the great central theme of historical development. Such is the historiographical background to the mid- and later Victorian preoccupation with the problems of constitutional history, and, in the field of seventeenth-century studies, the pinpointing of the constitutional conflict as the centrally important issue, and the concentration on the purely constitutional dimensions of phenomena such as the impositions, the patents of monopoly and Ship-money, usually to the neglect of their economic aspects, without which, as most historians of today would claim, even their purely constitutional aspects cannot properly be appreciated. Of course, another Victorian preoccupation, the vitally important connection between religion and the political struggle was not neglected by historians, least of all by Samuel Rawson Gardiner, whose multi-volume work is still the greatest modern account of the political history of the period. But while in the later Victorian period historians such as James Thorold Rogers and Archdeacon William Cunningham were at work laying some of the foundations of scientific economic history, and despite the fact that Cunningham was setting his economic materials within what some of his later critics were to consider a somewhat procrustean framework of institutions and royal policies familiar to political historians,[2] the initial impact of the new economic history on interpretations of the political history of the seventeenth century was minimal. Ultimately, however, the remarkable growth of a quasi-autonomous economic history has been one of the factors responsible for the changed emphasis which has marked many twentieth-century interpretations of the Civil War, even though the fact that the bulk of the practitioners of economic history have increasingly drawn their inspiration from economics and the social sciences rather than from history has meant that the reinterpretation of political history in the light of their findings has been left to their political and constitutional colleagues. Nevertheless, it is the obvious relevance of the material which researches into economic history have brought to light which has unquestionably provided a major incentive to such reinterpretations. It is true that during the nineteenth century Marx and his successors had been at pains to emphasise the essentially materialistic basis of all political revolutions, but so far as academic history was concerned, Marx was an eccentric and oddball figure. Among the many factors which have rendered Marxist interpretations – and those reactions against them which have a no less fundamentally materialistic basis – of enormously greater influence in the twentieth century is the collapse, as a result of two devastating world wars, of belief in the inevitability of progress, while the growth of totalitarian movements in Europe between the wars, and in the new nations of Asia and Africa after the second world war, has sapped our faith in the certainty of the triumph of representative institutions. To the mid-nineteenth-century 'liberal' mind it seemed that the idea of representative government was almost everywhere on the offensive against the forces of autocracy and legitimism. In our own time the nature of many of the régimes which have emerged from the overthrow of traditionalist states has shown this optimism to be ill founded. Meanwhile, in Britain and elsewhere, the achievement of political democracy was followed by demands for, and substantial progress towards, social democracy, a development which, while it may have helped to demonstrate the falsity of Marxist predictions about the increasing misery of the working class and the impossibility of social improvement without social revolution, has also been an important factor in focusing the attention of historians both upon material factors *per se* and upon the relationship between economic and political phenomena.

II

To the Marxist historian the Civil War represents the necessarily violent outcome of a century of capitalist growth.[3] From the later years of Elizabeth's reign the *bourgeoisie* had been outgrowing the leading-strings in which it had run with reasonable contentment during the Tudor period. With the worst dangers both of foreign conquest and of the usurpation of power by malcontent recusant noblemen now past, the *bourgeoisie* was becoming increasingly irritated by the restrictionist nature of many royal policies. It was not simply that such policies imposed restrictions on the freedom of economic enterprise. In addition to this was the fact that they were flawed by a fatal ambivalence of motive which in itself is very important in the widening division between Court and Country. On the one hand there was the government's sincere desire to regulate the economy in the interests of the well-being of the mass of the people. On the other there was its need to reward courtiers and officials, while lacking adequate funds to do so in ready cash. The Stuarts had courtiers whom they delighted to honour and officials whom they needed to reward. They also presided over a highly complicated system of economic controls, while lacking the ready cash for the remuneration of the professional salaried civil service which might have rendered such controls effective. The temptation to try to kill these two very different birds with the same stone – that is, to make rewards by granting to private persons what we should today regard as public rights of supervision and regulation in the hope that they would both employ them for the common benefit and make a substantial profit for themselves was too great to be resisted.

But to use such privileges both as a means of reward and as a means of executing social and economic policy was to pursue mutually incompatible aims. What might – and often did – happen can be illustrated by an example – the use of the aulnage of the new draperies, granted in the early years of James I's reign to the Duke of Lennox. A complicated set of ordinances and statutes regulated the length, breadth and quality of the traditional cloths manufactured in England. Similar, though less complicated, regulations applied to the new draperies – those cloths whose manufacture had been introduced into England during Elizabeth's reign by Flemish and Walloon immigrants, refugees from the religious persecutions of Alva and the Spaniards. The aulnager was the officer responsible for their enforcement, and on being satisfied that the cloth conformed to the statutory requirements, he (or his deputy) affixed his seal to it. But Lennox was not especially interested in the efficient observation of statutory regulations on the quality and size of cloth. He was in business for profit and he quickly found that he could maximise his gains by selling the aulnage seals in advance to the manufacturers of cloth, who then affixed them themselves.[4] Such illustrations of the incompatibility of the twin aims of government policy *vis-à-vis* economic and social regulations – on the one hand their efficient enforcement, and, on the other, their use as a substitute for rewards in cash – could be multiplied almost indefinitely.[5]

Marxist historians are probably right to stress the fact that a government which worked on such principles was likely to antagonise many Stuart businessmen. The existence of a clumsy and stifling (however well-intentioned) code of economic controls which had been built up over a century – and sometimes much longer – would in any case have aroused their hostility. But when such regulations had the additional purpose of serving as a form of out-relief for courtiers and government servants, it was more or less inevitable that they should come to be viewed as yet another device whereby the country was bled white by the court.

Of course, the reality is a great deal more complex than the foregoing passage might suggest. For although the majority of English business-men were irritated by these controls and their exploitation for the benefit of courtiers and royal servants, a small but powerful minority of them stood to gain. The opportunities, which they were quick to exploit, arose out of the fact that the courtly holders of economic concessions – of patents of monopoly, patents conferring rights of regulation in econ-omic matters, farms of the royal customs, and export licences, to cite but a few examples – rarely had either the expertise or the inclination to exploit them directly. Their normal practice was to sublet at a profit, either to individual businessmen or to syndicates of businessmen, who thus came to acquire a vested interest in the existing system. Similar arguments are applicable to another form of royal economic concession, the area monopolies of foreign trade granted to the great chartered companies. These were also the product of a doubtful amalgam of considerations of royal financial advantage and the imagined economic benefit of the realm in general, although the former consideration loomed less large than in the case of domestic concessions. While such commercial privileges were implacably opposed by the vast majority of English merchants who were excluded from their benefits, those who were fortunate enough to be members of such companies naturally took a different view of the situation. Thus what may be termed the court concessionary interest consisted not only of the courtier-concessionaries themselves, but also of a small but powerful minority of big businessmen who had everything to gain from the continuance of the system.

But persons who were engaged directly in industry and commerce were a small minority of the political nation in pre-industrial England,[6] in which circumstances, if the Marxist historian is to prove that the Civil War was fundamentally a material struggle, it will be necessary for him to extend his analysis into what was, in quantitative terms, the most important sector of the English economy. In the forefront of agricultural progress, as well as of opposition to royal policies, he places those landowners whose estates were efficient and up-to-date units of business management, whether they were farmed directly by their owners or whether their economies were based on modernised rent rolls which ensured that rents and fines responded sensitively to fluctuations in prices. Conversely, the main source of support for the Crown came from those 'backward' landowners whose relations with their tenants were based on outmoded paternalistic notions, who continued to maintain 'hospitality', and whose slackness and inefficiency provided golden opportunities for the improvement of the economic fortunes of another important agency of agrarian capitalism, those yeomen farmers who profited from lenient and outdated renting policies. At the same time the Crown, by not relaxing its inherited Tudor restrictions on the free use of their estates by landowners and, more specifically, by its retention of Tudor anti-enclosure legislation long after the political dangers which this legislation had been designed to counter had ceased to be of any real significance,[7] was at one and the same time hampering the 'progressive' landowner, who was prevented from putting his land to its most economic use, and protecting the 'backward', old-fashioned and inefficient landowner by cushioning him against the competition of more efficient and ruthless competitors. In the sphere of agrarian relations, therefore, the conflict of interest between backward- and forward-looking landowners represents, in Marxist terms, nothing less

than a clash between two utterly different and fundamentally opposed
ways of life. Herein lies the distinction, in agrarian terms, between
feudal and capitalistic modes of production. For when the Marxist
historian refers to 'feudal' landowners he does not mean to imply that
such landowners necessarily drew a preponderant – or even a significant – portion of their incomes from labour services compulsorily
exacted from unfree tenants as a part of their rent, or from personal
seigneurial dues which were rendered to landowners by virtue of their
feudal superiority. An economy which is characterised as 'feudal' in
Marxist terms may contain both or either of these characteristics. On the
other hand, it may not. For example, it clearly refers to the first of them
when used to characterise large areas of eastern Europe, which had
witnessed an intensification of predial services in the later Middle Ages,
a tendency which was accentuated by the growth of the international
grain trade in the later sixteenth and early seventeenth centuries.
Similarly, its use in connection with pre-revolutionary France might be
said to reflect another classic characteristic of feudalism, since the
exaction of personal seigneurial dues remained a central feature of the
economy of many French landowners down to 1789. But the Marxist
use of the term 'feudal' to characterise pre-Civil War England would
obviously be unacceptable if it were to be construed in this restricted
sense, for both predial services and seigneurial dues had virtually
disappeared from the English scene during the century which succeeded
the Black Death. In other words, while the Marxist historian would
probably regard the basic attitudes and way of life of backward-
looking landowners in early Stuart England as an inheritance from a
time when labour services and personal dues had prevailed,[8] he would
not regard the actual presence of such services and dues as a necessary
feature of a feudal society. To him feudalism is simply 'a form of society
in which agriculture is the basis of economy and in which political
power is monopolised by a class of landowners. The mass of the population consists of dependent peasants subsisting on the produce of their
family holdings. The landowners are maintained by the rent paid by the
peasants, which might be in the form of food or labour, as in early days,
or (by the sixteenth century) in money.'[9]

But although we can agree that this less restrictive definition of
feudalism allows of its applicability to early seventeenth-century no less
than to thirteenth-century England – not to speak of sixteenth-century
Pomerania or France – without doing violence to the nature of any of
these societies, the widening of the scope of what is understood by

'feudalism' raises other questions. For to accept this definition is immediately to ask whether in fact the Civil War can be said to have changed anything fundamentally, for post-Restoration England remained a society whose economic basis was in agriculture, and political power continued to be vested in the hands of a landowning class drawing rents from a dependent tenantry. In face of these facts, what remains of the Civil War as a classic exemplification of the thesis that 'force is the midwife of every old society pregnant with a new one'? To these objections the Marxist historian might reply by emphasising that it was the progressive landowners – a sort of agrarian wing of the *bourgeoisie* – who triumphed as a result of the Civil War, and the backward landowners who went under; and that even those royalist landowners who regained their lands either at the Restoration or during the Interregnum[10] were forced by economic circumstances to adopt more efficient ways of managing them; in a word, that although politics remained dominated by a class of landowners both before and after 1649, the fundamental economic outlook of this ruling class changed, and can more or less be equated with that of those landowners who had opposed the Crown in 1642. But we need to know a great deal more about English landed society in the later seventeenth century before we can accept this view, and even if we were ultimately to accept it, it is still arguable that the Civil War and the redistribution of landed wealth which followed it did little more than hasten a development which would have been achieved without recourse to armed conflict. This is, of course, not to deny that such factors may have played a part in the alignment of forces in 1642 but simply to suggest doubts about their primacy as determinants of the course of events. And to the Marxist the fundamental considerations which govern men's outlook towards the great issues of the day, the constitutional disputes, the Puritan challenge to the hierarchy, and the Laudian challenge to the Puritans, are to be found in his position *vis-à-vis* such material factors. In general, conservatives in economic practice will be conservative in social outlook and political and religious opinion. The Marxist historian would readily agree with Macaulay and the Whig historians of the nineteenth and twentieth centuries that the seventeenth century has a unique significance in English history as the period which saw the final and irreparable defeat of royal absolutist ambitions and the triumph of representative institutions. But probing beneath these surface phenomena, he claims to have found their true significance in their connection with the growth of capitalism, its requirement of greater space in which to breathe and expand still further and the final dawning of consciousness that this space can be created only by a revolution which will bring the whole superstructure of the existing régime down in ruins.

This article is concerned with the problem of the origins of the Civil War and not with the events of the years after 1642. But it is obvious that the same sort of Marxist analysis can be – and indeed has been – applied to these events, and not least to the divisions which arose between those opposing the Crown. It has been applied to the distinction between Presbyterians and Independents, while the fact that the more revolutionary political ideas of more radical groups such as the Levellers and the Diggers were never put into effect is in no way inimical to the Marxist thesis. For even if it could be demonstrated conclusively that the Levellers, for example, stood for political reforms which amounted to a great deal less than manhood suffrage,[11] this would not disprove the notion that, given the social and economic structure of seventeenth-century England, the achievement of their objectives was incompatible with those of a true bourgeois revolution. For the Marxist theory of the role of the bourgeois state during this stage of historical development, when the proletarisation of the industrial small master and the agricultural smallholder was still in its infancy, demands the intermission of a long period of savagely repressive legislation as a means of conditioning the gradually emerging working class to a state of mind in which it 'looks upon the conditions of that mode of production as self-evident laws of nature'.[12] Only when this has been achieved – and even then, only slowly and cautiously, a matter perhaps of centuries rather than decades – can such radical demands for electoral reform be seriously entertained. For the time being, political and social radicalism might be safely disregarded once the task of defeating the king had been successfully accomplished.

III

The idea of religious, political and constitutional issues as an ideological superstructure based on a foundation of material and class interests has been influential far beyond the ranks of Marxist historians. It has indeed been adopted, in part at least and with a radically different emphasis, by some of their more formidable and determined opponents. The following passage from a celebrated article by Professor Trevor-Roper may serve to remind us that anti-Marxist history is not necessarily history which plays down the crucial importance of material factors and class interest:

> Hit by the price revolution, slow to redeem their losses by 'good husbandry', left in the provinces from which, they complained, the hated metropolis had drained the wealth and vitality, taxed to maintain 'the expenses of a court so vast and unlimited by the old good rules of economy', the English mere gentry felt themselves to be a depressed, declining class, and, grumbling, consoled – or armed – themselves with religious dissent. Against a protestant court some of them struck under the banner of recusancy; against a 'popish' court others struck again, under the banner of puritanism.[13]

Professor Trevor-Roper is here emphasising the suitability of certain religious beliefs as the ideology of the 'outs', those 'mere gentry' who were excluded from that access to office which, in his view, provided the most important extra-agricultural source of income without which few gentry landowners could hope to improve their economic fortunes, given the socially compulsive need to engage in conspicuous expenditure and to 'maintain their port'.[14] In the Marxist view the Civil War was the revolt of the economically rising and progressive elements in society, infuriated by the restrictions which a conservative régime was imposing upon their economic advancement; in the view of Professor Trevor-Roper, the most dynamic element among the forces opposed to Charles I in the Civil War was to be found amongst groups who were, if anything, experiencing economic decline, and who desperately needed the income from office to shore up their tottering personal economies. The differences between the two views are, of course, enormous; so enormous that it is easy to forget that they hold in common the assumption that it is impossible to explain the real nature of the revolutionary movements of the seventeenth century without penetrating below the surface of conventional political and religious history,[15] and, more specifically, that it was vital to the economic interest of an important social group to overthrow the existing régime and seize power.

The weight which both schools of thought have attached to what might be described as the multi-dimensional character of the central issues of the conflicts of this period can be exemplified by their views about Puritanism.[16] The Weberian connection between Puritanism and Capitalism, operating, *inter alia*, via the Puritan emphasis on the disciplinary value of diligence in one's worldly calling and abstinence in the expenditure of the fruits of this diligence, is obviously grist to the

Marxist mill. While Professor Trevor-Roper sharply challenges the validity of this alleged connection, he does not question the value of such attempts to search out the extra-religious dimensions of religious phenomena. Indeed, he offers the alternative explanation that Puritanism was a creed which was better suited to the poor gentleman seeking to make ends meet than to the rich capitalist saving to invest.[17] And the two notions are by no means mutually exclusive. A declining gentleman might be attracted by a creed which enabled him to make a virtue out of the necessity of economic retrenchment, not least because it contrasted the exercise of this 'country' virtue with courtly luxury and vice. Similarly, the thriving capitalist might embrace with enthusiasm doctrines which stressed the theological merit of the unglamorous attributes whose exercise had provided the basis of his business success.

The other central issue of the period to which historians traditionally have attached most weight is, of course, the constitutional issue. On the question of the connection between religious belief and the constitutional struggle the historians of the twentieth century have added little to the work of their predecessors, such as S. R. Gardiner, who laid great stress on matters such as the Laudian advocacy of the doctrine of non-resistance and the way in which the Puritans had perforce to challenge existing authority and ally with the growing opposition to the Stuarts in parliament. Perhaps the most exciting scope for the further examination of this connection is now to be found in its manifestations at the all-important level of county affairs and the role of local Puritans *vis-à-vis* the encroachment of the central government in a wide variety of ways upon time-honoured local ways of doing things. And while conceding that Puritanism was indeed one of the seedbeds of modern liberalism, it is important not to allow this to obscure the fact that there was nothing inevitable about this connection, which resulted, not from the tenets of Puritanism *per se*, but from a highly complex concatenation of historical circumstances. Certainly, there is nothing inherently liberal about Puritan beliefs, and we might well ask whether they would have acquired the political connotations which we associate with them if the Stuart kings had themselves been Puritans. It is salutary to remind oneself that in the Netherlands the Arminians (or Remonstrants) were those who opposed the extension of the power of the Stadholder, while the strictly Calvinist Counter-Remonstrants were the allies of the House of Orange.

Circumstances alter cases. And just as there may be links between religious beliefs and economic interests, and between religious and

constitutional controversies, so the circle may be completed by emphasising the economic dimensions of some of the constitutional controversies
of the period. The assault on the Prerogative has familiar religious
connotations; it was prerogative courts which punished Puritan dissidents,
who sawed off the ears of Prynne, Burton and Bastwick. It was the same
prerogative courts which punished enclosing landlords, usurers, and
businessmen who defied patents of monopoly. It was from the exercise of
one of the most important of the Crown's prerogatives, the dispensing
power, that there flowed those patents and licences which so irritated
the business community. It was by virtue of his prerogative that the
king laid those extra-parliamentary impositions on trade which played
such an important part in the formation of both constitutional and
business opposition to the early Stuarts. Puritanism, constitutional
opposition and business opposition were all assaulting the same citadel.
The more their paths converged, the more intimate the connection
between them was likely to become. It would be absurd to suggest that
constitutional ideas *per se* could have attracted such wide support if they
had not been intimately connected with men's material interests.

During the great economic depression of the early 1620s the great
chartered companies, which owed their dominance and quasi-mono-
polistic position in so many branches of English foreign trade to royal
grants and protection, were subjected to violent attacks from parliaments which also showed themselves to be highly critical of numerous
other aspects of royal policy.[18] It would not be unreasonable to assume
that the sympathies of many of the members of such companies – men
who knew very well on which side their bread was buttered – would lie
with the Court rather than the Country. But of how many of them could
this be said in 1642? The lines of distinction between Court and Country
were shifting and blurred rather than static. The Long Parliament, which
was so violent in its denunciation of Arminian High Church practices,
of prerogative courts, of customs farmers and of holders of patents of
monopoly, was – in contrast to its predecessors of 1604, 1621 and 1624 –
strangely quiet when it came to the restrictive practices of the chartered
companies in foreign trade. This is surely a significant fact, and, in
seeking to explain it, two problems in particular call for investigation.
The first is the progressive weakening of the purely economic links
which bound the privileged class of exporters – the commercial élite
of the day – to Crown and Court, during the period between James I's
last parliament and the summoning of the Long Parliament by his
successor in 1640.[19] The second is their concurrent *rapprochement* with

parliament, about which little is known, but in which, I suspect, the history of the early parliaments of Charles's reign may well turn out to be crucial.[20] The events with which every schoolboy is familiar – the disputes over tonnage and poundage, the widespread refusal of influential merchants to pay duties, were events which have an economic as well as a constitutional dimension. In these years constitutional theories became woven into a fabric of business opposition, and, like the religious factors we have mentioned, acquired an extra-constitutional significance which gave to them a potency which they could never have had alone. For who cares about constitutional theories *per se* except the dry-as-dust? Taxpayers do not care the more for taxes simply on account of their constitutionality. 'No taxation without representation' does not mean that people would be quite happy with unlimited taxation provided it was granted constitutionally. Representation interests 99 out of every 100 of them because it will limit the level of taxation, since representatives are presumably responsive to the wishes of their constituents. Constitutional ideas are politically important in direct proportion as they are rooted in material realities.

But when they are thus rooted, they acquire a significance of their own. When men persuade themselves that actions which they take because it suits their pockets to take them are in fact taken for motives which are the reverse of self-seeking, it is possible that the myth may acquire a reality of its own. I would go further, and suggest that this process is as essential to the successful realisation of an ideology as is the fact that it is also rooted in material interests. Men come to believe in the ideology which they have subconsciously adopted because of its apparent harmony with their material interests. That they would not have adopted it without this harmony is an essential part of the argument. But no less essential is the complementary argument that this opposition would not have been the vital force it was if concepts of self-interest had not been subtly transmuted by the ideological alchemy of constitutional and religious beliefs. 'You've never had it so good' would not have been a viable political slogan in seventeenth-century England.

IV

The Marxists and the most effective and stimulating of their opponents have taught us that in seeking to explain the causes of the Civil War we cannot afford to neglect either the extra-religious dimension of religion or the extra-constitutional dimensions of the constitutional conflicts of the period. But we must beware of flying to the other extreme and must realise that the traffic of influence flows in both directions, for to fail to do this is to miss more than half of the significance of the events we are studying. To explain the issues over which Englishmen spilt one another's blood, including the blood of their king, solely in terms of thwarted economic ambitions is to oversimplify these issues at least as much as if we had left such considerations completely out of our analysis. It is to lower the political temperature, to discount religious enthusiasm and passionately felt religious antagonisms, and to reduce the springs of political action in 1640 to the level of those operating at the time of the accession of George III. It is to resuscitate the unimaginative crudities of eighteenth-century rationalist historians such as David Hume who were unable or unwilling to penetrate to the heart of the aspirations of men with whom they were entirely out of sympathy. For, at bottom, the importance of the extra-religious dimensions of religious issues in the seventeenth century is testimony not to the secondary importance of religion as a mere reflection of more fundamental factors, but to its crucial significance as something penetrating every aspect of man's activity. We may grant that the Puritanism of many opponents of the Stuarts owed something – how much will vary from one individual to another – to their exclusion from the varied benefits which flowed from one form or another of connection with the Court:

> Such as are not graced in a state
> May for their ends be adverse in religion
> And get a tune to call the flock together.[21]

But not all Puritans were Puritans because they were 'out'; some, and perhaps a majority, were 'out' because they were Puritans. Such a man was the Puritan peer, Lord Say and Sele, described by Clarendon as 'a man of a close and reserved nature, of a mean and narrow fortune, of great parts and of the highest ambition, but whose ambition would not be satisfied with offices and preferment without some condescensions and alterations in ecclesiastical matters'.[22] There were many like him, just as there were many others who were drawn towards Puritanism by grievances which we would today regard as being non-religious in character. Among the latter were businessmen who resented the obstacles to the achievement of their economic ambitions which were imposed by government regulations whose original *raison d'être* had been perverted by their use as a means of rewarding fashionable hangers-on at Court. Similarly, the impoverished country gentleman who observed, with feelings compounded of jealousy and disgust, the style of life which his more opulent neighbours were able to maintain with the aid of incomes swollen as a result of their court connections, might find in Puritanism ideological solace and a vehicle which helped to make his indignation appropriately righteous.

But it is not unlikely that he found a great deal more than this, and that Puritanism in its turn contributed something of its own to the character of the rift between Court and Country in the contrast which it drew between the pious and abstemious way of life deemed appropriate to the faithful and the ostentation, luxury and scandals of the Court with its unsavoury *causes célèbres* such as the Essex Divorce, the Lake scandals and the Overbury murder. It is true that in seeking the reasons which impelled men to take sides in the Civil War we can no longer afford to take the starry-eyed view of political motivation which characterised our Whig ancestors. But the sort of explanation which will suffice for the Essex Revolt or the Fronde will be insufficient to account for the Great Rebellion or the French Revolution. The great issues of the struggles of the seventeenth century are significant first and foremost because although they do in some measure represent ideologies of competing economic interests, these interests are in turn influenced, and sometimes transformed, by the religious and political doctrines which they espouse. In this intimate and two-way connection between interests and ideologies are to be found some of the most important clues to the solution of the problem not so much of why a Hampden, a Falkland or a Cromwell took a stand on these issues, but why they evoked a significant response in the hearts and minds of their less idealistic, less gifted and less politically conscious countrymen.

SHORT BIBLIOGRAPHY

It would be misleading to give a short bibliography in connection with the discussion of the causes of the English Civil War. The reader is referred to the bibliographies attached to the other chapters in this book, and those in *The English Revolution 1600–1660*, ed. E. W. Ives (1968) and in Ivan Roots, *The Great Rebellion*.

NOTES

1. H. R. Trevor-Roper, 'The Social Origins of the Great Rebellion', *History Today*, v (1955) 382.

2. For a characteristic questioning of Cunningham's emphasis, see G. Unwin, *Studies in Economic History*, ed. R. H. Tawney (1927) pp. 117–32.

3. For a short and lucid version of the Marxist interpretation, see Christopher Hill, *The English Revolution 1640* (1955 ed.). For some second thoughts, see his Recent Interpretations of the Civil War' in *Puritanism and Revolution* (1958) pp. 3–31.

4. W. H. Price, *The English Patents of Monopoly* (Cambridge, Mass., 1906) p. 27; W. R. Scott, *The Constitution and Finance of English, Scottish and Irish Joint Stock Companies* (Cambridge, 1912) i 138, 173; E. Lipson, *The Economic History of England*, 4th ed. (1947) iii 354.

5. See, for example, Price, op. cit., *passim*; L. Stone, *An Elizabethan: Sir Horatio Palavicino* (Oxford, 1956) pp. xiv–xvi and *passim*; R. H. Tawney, *Business and Politics under James 1* (Cambridge, 1958) esp. pp. 80–1, 85–90; A. F. Upton, *Sir Arthur Ingram* (1961) *passim*; R. Ashton, 'Charles 1 and the City' in *Essays in the Economic and Social History of Tudor and Stuart England in Honour of R. H. Tawney*, ed. F. J. Fisher (Cambridge, 1961) pp. 140–1; M. Prestwich, *Cranfield: Politics and Profits under the Early Stuarts* (Oxford, 1966) *passim*.

6. This is not to deny the growing importance of commercial interests among people who, while not engaging in commerce, took advantage of the growth of opportunities for commercial investment provided by the growth of joint-stock enterprise in this period. On this, see Theodore K. Rabb, 'Investment in English Overseas Enterprise, 1575–1630', *Econ. Hist. Rev.*, 2nd ser., xix (1966) 70–81; *Enterprise and Empire: Merchant and Gentry Investment in the Expansion of England, 1575–1630* (Cambridge, Mass., 1967) *passim*.

7. For a lucid and concise contemporary description of these dangers, see Francis Bacon's essay, 'Of Seditions and Troubles'.

8. On the importance of this sort of reasoning in Marxist thought, see E. R. A. Seligman, *The Economic Interpretation of History* (New York, 1961 ed.) p. 64.

9. Hill, op. cit., p. 4. Some of the arguments used in this section are adapted from those employed in my 'Cavaliers and Capitalists', *Renaissance and Modern Studies*, v (1961) 158–9.

10. On this subject see Joan Thirsk, 'The Sales of Royalist Land during the Interregnum', *Econ. Hist. Rev.*, 2nd ser., v (1952) 188–207; and her 'The Restoration Land Settlement', *JMH* xxvi (1954) 315–28. For a careful and most valuable study of the effect of the Civil War on the structure of landownership, see H. J. Habakkuk, 'Landowners and the Civil War', *Econ. Hist. Rev.*, 2nd ser., xviii (1965) 130–51.

11. Not every historian would go all the way with Professor C. B. Macpherson, in his denial of the democratic nature of Leveller aspirations. [C. B. Macpherson, *The Political Theory of Possessive Individualism* (Oxford, 1962) ch. iii.] For a different view, see J. C. Davis, 'The Levellers and Democracy', *PP* no. 40 (1968) 174–80. For a very recent, short and admirable balanced essay on the Levellers, see Brian Manning, 'The Levellers' in *The English Revolution*, ed. Ives, pp. 144–57. This last volume provides an excellent introduction to some of the main problems of the period.

12. Karl Marx, *Capital*, tr. Samuel Moore and Edward Aveling, ed. Friedrich Engels (1946 ed.) p. 761. At this stage of development, argues Marx, the *bour-*

geoisie 'wants and uses the power of the state to "regulate" wages, *i.e.* to force them within the limits suitable for surplus-value making, to lengthen the working day, and to keep the labourer himself in the normal degree of dependence. This is an essential element of the so-called primitive accumulation' (ibid., pp. 761–2).

13. H. R. Trevor-Roper, 'The Gentry 1540–1640', *Econ. Hist. Rev.*, Supplement, no. 1 (n.d.) 52–3.

14. For some criticisms of this view, see Ashton, *Renaissance and Modern Studies*, loc. cit., pp. 159–63.

15. Cf. the Marxist views on this subject with Professor Trevor-Roper's statements on the primacy of social causes in his brilliant article, 'The General Crisis of the Seventeenth Century', *PP* no. 16. (1959) espec. p. 34.

16. For some observations on this subject, see my 'Puritanism and Progress', *Econ. Hist. Rev.*, 2nd ser., xvii (1965) 582–3.

17. Trevor-Roper, *History Today*, loc. cit., p. 379; cf. 'The Gentry 1540–1640', pp. 30–1, and *PP*, loc. cit., p. 60.

18. See, for example, A. Friis, *Alderman Cockayne's Project and the Cloth Trade* (1927) pp. 395-413, 428–31; B. E. Supple, *Commercial Crisis and Change in England 1600–1642* (Cambridge, 1959) pp. 62–4, 68–72.

19. On this see my 'Charles I and the City' in *Essays . . . in Honour of R. H. Tawney,* ed. Fisher, pp. 149–59.

20. This subject will be treated in my forthcoming book on early Stuart London.

21. Ben Johnson, *The Alchemist*, Act III, Sc. ii.

22. Clarendon, *History of the Rebellion*, (ed. W. D. Macray); i 241.

7. Interest – Public, Private and Communal

IVAN ROOTS

THE crown under Charles I, particularly during the so-called 'personal government' from 1629 to 1640, has often been seen as standing against all private and sectional interests for the maintenance of something labelled variously by contemporaries or historians 'the public interest', 'the common good', 'the welfare of England', 'the commonweal', 'the commonwealth', 'the interest of the kingdom'. The king, who was so good to his own children, can be seen as a sort of father-figure, *pater patriae*, a benevolent, impartial force checking oligarchy, conspiracy by rich or malevolent men – sometimes both – to endanger social stability. He becomes the protector of society against its own worst enemy, itself. Such a king deserves to be accorded a divine right – apart from any other arguments that can be produced 'out of *Gods booke*' that 'the *Authority* of a *King* . . . is the natural and essential investment of his Person . . . [which is] *Gods anointed*'[1] – because he has undertaken a divine responsibility. He is like the keystone of the arch of government or society, not an ornament merely – though he was that, too – but fulfilling a unique, practical and necessary function. This is, of course, the burden of Wentworth's much-quoted speech at the end of 1628 to the Council of the North, a more or less eloquent expression of a view that must have been a commonplace to his hearers.[2]

The claim to be saviour of society had historical and legal backing – by the law of the land, the law of nature, the law of God, and whatever. It had also a *de facto* support in that the monarch did control the executive, devise and call for the implementation of policies – something he had done time out of mind. But by the sixteen-thirties a share in the expression of the public interest was bid for by others, coming forward when opportunity offered as public trustees, hinting that they could represent the commonweal as well or even better than a crown liable in recent experience at least to be misled by evil or ignorant advisers. This rival – or would-be partner – was, of course, parliament, more directly representative, it might be asserted, of 'the interest of England' than the crown which could be considered to represent ultimately nothing but

itself. Parliament embraced directly the peerage and the commons was
however imperfectly a reflection of the rest of the political nation. 'King-
in-Parliament' also took in the crown itself, merging its legitimate
interests with those of 'the people'. Could there be a more authoritative
embodiment of the commonweal than that? Henry VIII a century
before had, apparently, thought not.

Inquiries into the location of the shield of the public interest are in the
nature of things rarely academic. In the early seventeenth century the
arguments spilled over from abstract political theory – if there was such
a thing – into red-hot pamphlets, sermons, news-sheets, private correspondence, intimate conversation. They were the stuff of M.P.s' speeches,
legal causes and apprentices' slogans. They heated the atmosphere of
politics, contributing to the conflagration of the sixteen-forties. Whatever else it was – and it was, undeniably, many other things – the civil
war was a competition – or series of competitions – between different –
or changing – views of the nature, embodiment and habitation of the
public interest.

The very phrase 'the public interest' was a source of discord. Both
'public' and 'interest' were old and already complex words. Coming
together about this time, they added considerably to their semantic
content. Definition was, however, almost wilfully avoided. Many men
assumed or preferred to let it be assumed that the meaning was self-
evident, just as 'the fundamental laws' were. (*They* were not.) Henri,
duc de Rohan (1579–1638), the talented and respected Huguenot
disputant, described the public interest with awe as a distinct entity,
an abstraction that made itself known by its own mysterious but inexor-
able will. 'The ruler may deceive himself, his advisers may become
corrupt, but interest itself can never be at fault. According as it is
understood, well or ill, states may prosper or perish.'[3] No doubt this is
true, but it is questionable if de Rohan, who was influential among English theorists, really contributed anything substantial to the resolution of
what were serious practical problems. His views encouraged either the
by-passing of definition altogether or flabby definition – neither helpful
to English circumstances in this quizzical period.

Some – among them a few of the Levellers – who could not agree that
the public interest *was* self-evident claimed it could, however, be easily
established by 'right reason'. Men ought to be able to recognise it as
they recognised their own self-interest. This is at first glance a feasible
proposition. But could and did men in toils really sort out their self-
interest as simply and sharply as all that? Charles I no doubt saw his

actions as contributing to the realisation of his own interests but that he was wrong about them was amply demonstrated on a grim morning in January 1649 – unless he really was impelled throughout the sixteen-forties by a 'death-wish'.

If self-interest was unclear, it is hardly likely that the more remote public interest was more obvious. For some men it was the opposite of private interests. Many of Laud's and Strafford's remarks in their comforting correspondence suggest they thought this way – though other passages and a few of their actions speak otherwise. Strafford's speech of 1628, already referred to, stresses an essential interrelationship and Laud asserted that the individual could and should realise himself in society. Other men took a less ambiguous line. They saw the fulfil-ment of private interests as an essential, if not the only essential, contribution to the realisation of the common good. We are a stone's throw away from 'true self-love and social are the same' and hardly further from 'what's good for General Motors is good for the U.S.A.'. The point was reached at which a lack of private interests so far from being an advantage might be a positive danger to the fulfilment of the commonweal. Cromwell expressed one aspect of this attitude when at the Putney Debates he denied a political – indeed almost any social – role to men who had 'but the interest of breathing'.[4] Men with no stake in the country, unless restrained, would hold a stake to its heart. Another facet of this attitude is put by the obscure but emphatic John Hall of Richmond:

> . . . to dream of public-spirited persons or public souls (meaning such as have no private interest) is not only untrue, but could it be, it would instead of benefit, be the ruin of that whole state. For through the distracted endeavours of so many voluntary public undertakers, the whole would perish by degrees, and while each particular failed for want of due self-regard, the whole would fail by consequence.[5]

Rarely have 'do-gooders' been so roundly trounced.

Generally the notion of a simple dichotomy of public and private interests was rejected. Men plumped for an inevitable relationship, clear-cut for some, complicated for others. Strafford would not have the two unravelled because afterwards they could never be entwined properly again. Granted the relationship, the crown could be held to represent the public interest precisely because, devoid itself of private concerns, it could bring all interests together into a working unity. On the other hand it could just as precisely embody the public interest

best because it did have its own particular interests – family, dynastic
personal, institutional – very like those of the private citizen. In
protecting its own, the crown protects all other interests, severally or
jointly. The king has rights and prerogatives which are just like the
'liberties' of individual Englishmen. If his are weakened, so are all
other existing rights. The common good will be preserved by maintaining 'the private good ' of the crown. (There are, of course, glaring
difficulties in the way of advocates of this view. Does the *extension* of
these interests of the crown reinforce the public interest, or threaten
it?)

It could also be argued that 'a single person' was best for preserving
the common good because he has only one interest to push – his own.
Thus Charles offered in 1648 'a personal treaty' as the most feasible
way 'to satisfy all interests'. The advocate of 'the single person' could
also back his case by reference to the speed with which decisions could
be reached when only one interest had to be consulted, the secrecy that
could be more confidently assured and the valuable experience which
accrued when a conscientious king sat on the throne for a long time.
Ministers might come and go, parliaments be called, prorogued and
dismissed. In comparison kings stood for continuity and in a sense were
everlasting – 'The king is dead; long live the king!'

Assemblies, on the other hand, were likely to take in so many different
interests competing, each aiming at mastery, that the common good
could get lost in chaos. The fewer men that shared responsibility the
better. Harrington gave a lot of thought to this view when in the autumn
of 1659 under his very eyes England drifted towards political collapse.
He rejected the argument. Instead he asserted that 'a commonwealth . . .
must consist especially of such an Assembly, the result thereof,
can go upon no interest whatsoever, but that only which is the common
interest of the whole people.' This could only be a large assembly since
'an Assembly consisting of a few may go upon the interest of one man,
as a king, or upon the interests of one party, as that of Divines, lawyers
and the like, or the interest of themselves and the perpetuation of their
government. . . . The popular Assembly in a commonwealth may consist of too few, but can never consist of too many.' Since 'the highest
earthly Felicity that a People can ask, or GOD can give, is an equal and
well-ordered commonwealth . . . the whole People by their peculiar and
natural Right and Power, do institute and ordain their whole commonwealth. . . .'[6] A knowing and judicious people can find under certain
conditions the public interest for themselves.

There were as many disputes over the range of public interest as over its lodging. Some men were content to leave the whole thing a mystery revealed only to kings, who had no need to let their subjects in on the secret – indeed, it might be dangerous to attempt it. But most were prepared to plump for at least 'security against external enemies'. Others went on to make it 'security *plus*' – security together with one or some or all of the following: internal peace and order; the preservation of property; the preservation of liberties, even, perhaps, liberty; prosperity; social harmony; physical and/or moral welfare; the promotion of happiness. Each extension is a source of renewed argument, since each calls for definition and location of the powers to implement it. The wider the range and the looser the definition the more authority the exponents of public interest can justly claim. 'Security' suggests at least control of foreign policy and the raising of men and money to implement it, ship-money for instance. It may even speak for the levying of a standing army. 'Internal peace and order' might reinforce the case for such a standing force, would point to the need for a local militia under central control and in general back claims for the effective co-ordination and supervision of local government from the centre. 'Prosperity' calls for regulation of trade and industry, monopolies, apprentice regulation, impositions and so on. Ship-money, too, since the charge was associated with the aspirations of a Fishery Society. Establishment and maintenance of 'social harmony' implies a social and economic policy concerned to put into effect poor laws, wage and price regulations, sumptuary laws, market rules. 'Happiness' gives almost *carte blanche*. It could, for example, justify actions in prerogative and ecclesiastical courts to preserve and indeed extend the interests of women in face of the common law, that 'husband's law'. Here, then, was a happy hunting ground for disputants of all kinds – lawyers, politicians (conservative, moderate, radical, sincere, cynical), preachers, pamphleteers, political theorists and men of action. Their squabbles did not make civil war inevitable, but they contributed hugely to a situation in which by early 1642 it was possible, by late 1642 seemed unavoidable and by 1643 seemed more or less unstoppable.

'The public interest' and 'self-interest' are the two extremes of a wide spectrum, moving across from 'the nation' to the solitary individual. In between these two extremities there lies a wide area of other interests which were of practical concern to contemporaries and which cannot be ignored by the historian in his struggle to get under the skin of the age. Most of these interests can be associated with *communities* of many different types. The main entity, the British Isles, can be broken down into England, Wales, Scotland and Ireland, broad geographical and historical divisions, sharing some common interest but each with its own peculiar concerns. These were emphatically affected by and were themselves effecting changes in their relationships. The Acts of Union in the reign of Henry VIII did not and could not expunge uniquely Welsh interests; in fact they catered for some and created others. To make Irishmen into Englishmen, as Strafford seemed to want to do, was an impossibility, especially as the attempt was so obviously an aspect of the exploitation of Ireland in the interests of England as interpreted by Strafford. The Covenanters showed in the late 1630s how little the interests of Scotland had merged with those of England when James VI went south in 1603 to become also James I.

Each of these large territorial units was an agglomeration of lesser, but hardly less tenaciously upheld, communities. In England the provinces confronted the metropolis, each with a congeries of interests and attitudes. Within the provinces there were distinct regional communities such as the North. 'The far North' or border country had its own values and manners. There were communities such as the Fenlands, whose whole way of life was threatened, almost destroyed at this time by drainage operations, which could themselves be regarded as in the public interest. Conflicts here flared into violence and excited the concern of such different upholders of established rights and customs as Wentworth and Cromwell. The franchise of Durham and the Isle of Man were 'special cases', but the forty English counties each had a sense of community rooted both in the past and the present. Studies of Kent, Gloucestershire, Staffordshire, Suffolk, Nottingham and Somerset in this period have clinched the existence of the 'strange and introverted society of the county community' in which 'everything – religion, learning, law, politics, trade, even history itself – was formed and tempered by the bonds of local kinship and custom', giving 'shape to the infinite diversity of English provincial life'.[7] Similarly towns and cities – Newcastle-upon-Tyne, Exeter, Lincoln, Maidstone, even London itself[8] – had not merely a formal corporate existence backed by charters, but were living communities that could give rise to burning local patriotism. The military history – to say nothing of the political and social history – of the Interregnum was profoundly influenced by these feelings which ran counter to the pressures of dynamic exponents of what seemed to many not 'the good old cause' but a remote, incomprehensible one.

All these were communities with a fairly specific topographical placement, within borders defined by history or geography – a river, a wall, or line on a map or plan. But there were many other kinds of community existing alongside, within or cutting across these more tangible boundaries. None of them the historian can afford to overlook. A trawl with a wide net brings up 'the political nation'; parliament (looked at from one angle a single entity, from another seen to be at least three: king, lords and commons); the peerage (almost but never quite the same as the lords in parliament); the commonalty, a loose embodiment of a multiplicity of communities; the gentry (court, country, parochial); the yeomanry; 'the meaner sort of people' and whatever. The Church was one community in the sight of God and William Laud, but a world of separate, if loosely linked, bodies of common interest in the eyes of men: dioceses, parishes, chapters, clergy, laity. Outside the Church of England was the recusant community, itself capable of being anatomised or atomised into communities. Then there were the unconformable congregations proliferating in the sixteen-forties, provoking Thomas Edwards into the horridly fascinating compilation of *Gangraena*. Each would put forward its claims to be a community, some to being the nearest thing to a Christian community here on earth.

The Court was a community, so were the privy council and the various boards and departments of state. The courts – common law or prerogative – were communities, highly organised and articulate in the defence of their interests. Lawyers formed a genuine community, subscribing not merely to the perpetuation of their fees and perquisites but asserting the standards of their profession and its utility to the larger community of which they were also members. The universities were communities and within them the individual colleges were sodalities sometimes linked with communities in a wider world – Jesus College, Oxford with Wales, Exeter with the South-West. Schools were communities long before 'the old school tie' flaunted exclusiveness. Societies such as Gresham College and the various antiquarian and literary associations, formal and informal, London- or provincial-based, were genuine expressions of specific communal concerns.

Trades and professions – doctors of medicine, Turkey merchants, scriveners, midwives, theatrical companies (the list is endless)–were all in their various ways communities, some strictly confined by charters or statutes, with communal possessions, real or moveable, unique rites and ceremonies. Others were less clearly delineated. But all of them had acquired and were employing at least some of the paraphernalia of a living community: bonds of fellowship, a feeling of continuity – an awareness of a past, present and future. They were both inward- and outward-looking.

Can we stop here? What of the family of women and youth who even then could not live with crabbed age? What of the wayfarers to whom Professor Alan Everitt has recently directed our attention, connecting them up with developments in the economic, social and religious life of the larger community of England through which they wandered 'mobile, rootless and radical, questing in . . . ambitions and continually addicted to change'?[9] No doubt in the very nature of things the way-farers were more dynamic, but many of the other communities, too, deliberately or unwittingly contributed to the fluidity of the age. It has been pointed out that they often had a sense of continuity. This could mean conservatism, digging in. It could also foster enterprise, not merely to preserve the trust from the past but to improve the present and hand over something better to posterity. To exist might mean to to extend, to demand more to protect what was held already. (Is not this in fact what both crown and parliament were doing in the consti-tutional sphere? There is no clear line between revolution and reaction.)

All this is so obvious it need not have been said. Yet the obvious, as Poe pointed out in *The Purloined Letter*, goes often unnoticed. In trying to come to some conclusions about the public interest, or rather to start talking about it at all, the historian must contemplate these miscellaneous communities, as any individual must have done, con-sciously or unconsciously, when making decisions of the kind that interest the historian – such as taking sides in the civil war in 1642, subscribing to the engagement in 1650, refusing to serve as a commis-sioner under a major-general in 1656. Any individual faced with such a problem belonged as of course to any number of communities, and his view of his self-interest and of the public interest was coloured by his membership. John Doe, let us call him, was a provincial not a Londoner, a northerner not a south-westerner. He was a merchant in a small way, not a man of substance. He had grammar-school but not university training. He was a puritan but within the Church of England. He was middle-aged not young, at least he was in 1642. All of these qualities are individual but are involved in communities – all of them in various ways and strengths must have affected his decision in 1642. But move on to 1656 – he is no longer middle-aged but getting on, he has done well out of the war, left his provincial town and come to London, a fresh and wider community. He is a member of a chartered company, trading overseas. He has joined an independent congregation. He has married, has children. He is still John Doe but his membership of fresh communities has changed his views of self- and public interest. There are different forces operating on his decision-making.

So self-interest is not a fixed thing but has to be found by the individual and the historian again and again according to changing circumstances. Sometimes the fragments of interest which emerge from an individual's community memberships are (or at least appear to him to be) consistent, 'to jell', as it were. Then decision is easy. Sometimes they conflict, feel or are flatly contradictory. Then tension arises in the making of decision – and may prevent a positive one from being reached at all. Such community strains in self-interest help to explain the difficulty many men found in making up their minds in the stern crises of the seventeenth century, in becoming royalists or roundheads or both or neither. It suggests why some men were moderates today and extremists tomorrow. It accounts reasonably for the ease with which some men changed sides, why some catholics fought for the parliament, puritans for the king, some monopolists for parliament, some improving landlords for the king (who was, of course, on occasion one himself). No wonder the civil wars and what followed were a series of shocks, bewildering even to those who took the large decisions which forced other men to take up and review their own positions again and again. Oliver Cromwell would have been hard put to it to explain even to himself the motivations which pricked him time after time into decisive action after agonising bouts of apparent procrastination. The historian can hope to get some way towards understanding this difficult man only by looking into the whole rich complex of his community memberships. To label him 'squire' and/or 'backbencher' will not do. (That is rather like summing up Mr Enoch Powell as a Professor of Greek.) When Oliver was offered the crown in 1657 he was a Protector, an old man, an army commander, and more besides. In refusing kingship the whole lot played a part.

As individuals or units of society men are complex creatures. They were no less thick-textured in the early seventeenth century. We sometimes forget this. To prove that Strafford on a number of occasions fell below his expressed ideals is not at once to establish him as a hypocrite or 'a typical seventeenth-century careerist' (whatever that may mean). But it certainly lights up another facet of him, and reinforces what was already fairly clear: that he was a man at odds with himself as much as with other people, pulled awry by various interests, as he variously heeded them – self-, communal and public. He could recognise 'Lady Mora' at the Court of St James's because he had already met her and would meet her again in himself. Strafford's very style of writing and speaking – an odd mixture, hardly a blend, of the 'sad' and formal and the brisk and colloquial – reveals the man.

The shifting alignments of self- and communal interest in Strafford and Cromwell imply a fluidity in their interpretation of 'the public interest'. There was in fact no single entity that could be confidently put forward as *the* public interest. Rather there was an infinite range of them. The various régimes of the period glimpsed only a few of them; their critics glimpsed others. To say flatly that under Charles I the implementation of a social policy was 'in the public interest' is at once to say nothing and to say too much. His government aimed at social harmony (among other things), but in fact he disturbed it as much as he realised it. Local authorities resented the arrowy finger of Whitehall, enterprising men chafed under frustration all the more galling perhaps when they heard that the king was claiming merit as an improver for draining the fens.[10] There were sincere as well as venal complaints about the aims and the methods used – including the prerogative courts, once the engines of acceptable policies, now increasingly deplored. And all this is to say nothing of Tawney's 'trail of finance', a mile wide. As suggested above, controversy was whipped up even when the area accorded to the public interest was put at its narrowest – security. Security justified the overall ship-money writs which touched so many communal and individual interests – among them property, localism and legal procedures – about which not only John Hampden felt strongly.

Decisions taken, then, in the public interest were necessarily speculative. They could not hope to satisfy all the people – not even the limited people of 'the political nation' – all the time. However well-intentioned, they were always liable to arouse heats which could not be quenched by reference to 'the commonweal', 'salus populi' or any other traditional bromide. Rather the atmosphere grew hotter as the issues were canvassed by groups of people of diverse and shifting outlooks who, wanting to be 'knowing', were prepared to ask awkward questions. Students of the period may draw some conclusions from this. One is certainly the need for as much narrative, and as detailed, as possible. Another is to examine groups, parties, interests, communities as they were in flux and in relation to the narrative. The independents of 1646

were not the independents of 1649. Nor were the Levellers. Dr Brian
Manning has recently said of the Levellers that 'their ideas were
formed in the local communities in which they lived and worked'.[11] If
we drop the limiting epithet 'local' and understand 'community' in the
broad sense used above, this comment is apt for any group or individual.
To search for these communities and to evaluate their impact and relationships is to undertake a hard, if not impossible, journey. But the
historian, travelling hopefully, may remind himself of William Walwyn's
comment on another impossibility – the abolition of private property:
'We must endeavour it.'[12]

SHORT BIBLIOGRAPHY

Irene Coltman, *Private Men and Public Causes* (1962).
A. M. Everitt, *The Community of Kent and the Great Rebellion* (Leicester, 1966).
A. M. Everitt, *The Local Community and the Great Rebellion* (1969).
J. A. W. Gunn, *Politics and the Public Interest in the Seventeenth Century* (1969).
Christopher Hill, *Puritanism and Revolution* (1958).
R. Howell, Jr, *Newcastle upon Tyne and the Puritan Revolution* (Oxford, 1967).
E. W. Ives (ed.), *The English Revolution* (1968).
M. A. Judson, *The Crises of the Constitution* (New Brunswick 1949).
C. B. MacPherson, *The Political Theory of Possessive Individualism* (1962).*
H. R. Trevor-Roper, *Religion, The Reformation and Social Change* (1967).
C. V. Wedgwood, *Thomas Wentworth, 1st Earl of Strafford* (1961).

NOTES

1. Edward Symmons, *A Loyal Subjects Beliefe* (Oxford, 1643) pp. 1, 9.
2. Tanner *MSS* lxxii 300, printed by S. R. Gardiner in *The Academy* (June
1875).
3. Henri de Rohan, *De l'interest des princes et estats de la Chrestienté* (1643)
pp. 10–13, quoted (in a slightly different translation) in J. A. Clarke, *Huguenot
Warrior* (The Hague, 1966) p. 186.
4. Woodhouse (ed.), *Puritanism and Liberty* (1938 ed.) p. 59 ('The Putney
Debates', 29 October 1647).
5. John Hall, *Of Government and Obedience* (1654) p. 98, quoted in J. A. W.
Gunn, *Politics and the Public Interest in the Seventeenth Century* (1969) p. 98.
The first draft of this article has been revised in the light of a number of points
made in Mr Gunn's excellent study, which appeared shortly after it was written.
6. James Harrington, *Aphorisms Political*, 2nd enlarged ed. (12 September 1659)
nos. lxviii, lx, lxi, cxx and cxix. The *Aphorisms Political* deserve close attention.
In the eighteen days between the first (25 August) and the second editions

* See also J. C. Davis, 'The Levellers and Democracy', *PP* no. 11 (1968).

Harrington added forty-four aphorisms to the original sixteen and revised several others. The changes show him reacting swiftly but thoughtfully to the events of late summer 1659, particularly Booth's rising.

7. Alan Everitt, 'The County Community', pp. 62–3, in *The English Revolution* ed. Ives. This volume also contains articles by Ivan Roots on 'The Central Government and the Local Community' and D. H. Pennington on 'The County Community at War'.

8. See e.g. Pearl, *London and the Outbreak of the Puritan Revolution* (Oxford, 1961) and R. Howell, Jr, *Newcastle upon Tyne and the Puritan Revolution* (Oxford, 1967).

9. Everitt, 'County Community', pp. 59–62.

10. S. R. Gardiner (ed.), *Reports of Cases in the Courts of Star Chamber and High Commission* (Camden Society, 1886) p. 61 (Attorney-General *v.* Moody and others, 1631).

11. *Econ. Hist. Rev.*, 2nd ser., xxii, 1 (April 1969) 131: review of Don M. Wolfe (ed.), *Leveller Manifestoes of the Puritan Revolution* (reprint, 1967).

12. [John Price?], *Walwins Wiles* (1649) p. 13, reprinted in W. Haller and G. Davis (eds), *The Leveller Tracts 1647–1653* (N.Y., 1944), p. 302.

NOTES ON CONTRIBUTORS

ROBERT ASHTON has been a Professor of English History in the University of East Anglia since 1963. Before that he taught at Nottingham University and (for one year) at the University of California, Berkeley. He was a pupil of the late Professor R. H. Tawney and contributed an article on Charles I and the City to the *Festschrift* for Professor Tawney in 1961. Apart from occasional papers he is the author of *The Crown and the Money Market* (Oxford, 1960) and *James I by his Contemporaries* (London, 1969). He is at present working on a book on Early Stuart London and another on the origins of the English Civil War.

BRIAN MANNING was an Assistant Lecturer at King's College and a Commonwealth Fellow in the U.S.A. from 1957 to 1959 before becoming a Lecturer in History at the University of Manchester. During 1967 and 1968 he was visiting lecturer at All Souls, Oxford. He contributed an article on 'The Nobles, the People, and the Constitution' to *Crisis in Europe, 1560–1660*, edited by T. Aston, and another article on 'The Levellers' in *The English Revolution*, edited by E. W. Ives. He is at present writing a book on the parties in the English Civil War.

D. H. PENNINGTON was educated at The King's School, Macclesfield, and Balliol College, Oxford. He taught in the Department of History at Manchester University from 1946 to 1965, since when he has been a Fellow of Balliol College. His publications include *Members of The Long Parliament*, which he wrote with Dr Brunton, and *The Committee at Stafford, 1643–45* (with Ivan Roots) and *Seventeenth Century Europe*.

IVAN ROOTS was educated at Maidstone Grammar School and Balliol College, Oxford, where he obtained first-class honours in Modern History. He then lectured at University College, Cardiff, and during 1960–1 he was Visiting Professor at Layfayette College, Pennsylvania. Since 1967 he has been Professor of History at the University of Exeter. Apart from contributing to a number of books, he is author of *The Great Rebellion 1642–1660*, and editor, with D. H. Pennington, of *The Committee at Stafford 1643–45* and *Conflicts in Tudor and Stuart England*.

C. V. WEDGWOOD is the author of numerous books on English and European History in the period of religious wars, including *The Thirty Years War*, *William the Silent* and *Richelieu and the French Monarchy*. She has been engaged for a number of years on writing a sequence of volumes on the English Civil War, of which *The King's Peace* and *The King's War* have been published, and the final volume, *The English Republic*, is in preparation. She has for many years been a member of the Royal Commission on Historical Manuscripts, and has served on the Arts Council and as a trustee of the National Gallery. C. V. Wedgwood was educated in London, Bonn and Paris, and at Lady Margaret Hall, Oxford. For the past five years she has been Special Lecturer in History at University College London. She was honoured with the O.M. in 1969.

AUSTIN WOOLRYCH was educated at Westminster School and then served in tanks in the Western Desert before entering Pembroke College, Oxford, where he obtained first-class honours in History. He lectured at the University of Leeds until 1964, when he was appointed to the Chair of History at the University of Lancaster. His publications include *Battle of the English Civil War* and *Oliver Cromwell*. He is at present working on monographs on Barebone's Parliament, and a volume of the Yale Edition of Milton's Complete Prose.

Index

Acton, Sir William, 4
Adolphus, Gustavus, 6
Albemarle, Duke of, see Monck, George
Ashley Cooper, Anthony, Earl of Shaftesbury, 70
Astley, Sir Jacob, 29
Aston, John, 6
Axtell, Sir Jacob, 29

Barebone, Praise-God, 68–74, 83
Barkstead, John, Major-General, 83
Barrington, Sir Thomas, 14
Bastwick, John, 34, 105
Baxter, Richard, 4, 60, 65–6
Beale, Thomas, 5
Bedford, Earl of, 14
Berry, James, Major-General, 83, 85, 86
Blake, Robert, 70
Boteler, William, Major-General, 82, 83, 85, 86
Bower, Edward, 49
Bradley, Matthew, 30
Bradshaw, John, 48, 50–5
Bristol, Earl of, 31
Buckingham, Duke of, 25, 28
Burton, Henry, 34, 105

Canne, John, 74
Carlisle, Earl of, see Howard, Charles
Carew, John, 76
Charles I, 1, 3, 16, 22–5, 28, 31–9, 41–58, 60, 64, 78, 81, 93, 111–14, 119–20
Charles II, 70
Chillenden, Edmund, 68
Cholmley, Sir Hugh, 18
Clarendon, Earl of, see Hyde, Edward
Coke, Sir Edward, 24
Cony, George, 78–9
Cook, John, 45, 48, 49–50
Cornwallis, Sir Frederick, 4

Courtenay, Hugh, 76
Cranborne, Lord, 4
Crane, Sir Robert, 15
Crompton, Thomas, 84
Cromwell, Oliver, 38, 41, 43–5, 47, 52–7, 59, 62, 64, 66–76, 78–87, 108, 113, 116, 119
Culpepper, Sir John, 23, 33, 35
Cunningham, William, Archdeacon, 96

Davis, John, 4–5
Derby, Earl of, see Stanley, James
Dering, Sir Edward, 35
Desborough, John, Major-General, 71, 79, 81, 86
Downes, John, 54

Earle, Thomas, 4
Edwards, Thomas, 117
Eliot, Sir John, 24
Elizabeth I, 38
Essex, Earl of, 3, 31–2, 38
Eure, Lord, 70
Everitt, Professor Alan, 118

Falkland, Viscount, 31, 35, 108
Fairfax, Lady, 49, 53
Fairfax, Lord, 17–18
Fairfax, Sir Thomas (later Lord), 17–18, 43–4, 46, 49, 57, 62, 63, 67
Feake, Christopher, 65, 66, 74, 75–6
Filmer, Sir Robert, 94–5
Finch, John, 31

Gardiner, S. R., 68, 95–6, 104
Goffe, William, Major-General, 85
Grey, Lord, 46
Grimston, Harbottle, 14

Hall, John, 113
Hampden, John, 7, 26–7, 30, 31, 34, 78–9, 108, 120

Harley, Sir Robert, 5–6
Harley, Lady, 6
Harrington, James, 114
Harrison, Thomas, 42, 46, 57, 65–76
Haynes, Major-General, 84, 86
Herbert, Sir Edward, 31
Hertford, Marquis of, 16–17
Hewson, Colonel, 46
Hollis, Denzil, 12, 30, 31
Hotham, Sir John, 18, 23
Howard, Charles, Earl of Carlisle, 70
Hume, David, 107
Hutchinson, Colonel, 47
Hutchinson, Lucy, 47
Hyde, Edward, Earl of Clarendon, 16–
    17, 23, 29, 31, 33, 35–6, 69–70, 108

Ireton, Henry, 41, 44, 53, 57

James I, 24, 25, 38

Kelsey, Thomas, 79, 82, 83, 85, 86

Lambert, John, 66, 67, 70–2, 75, 80, 83
Lascelles, Francis, 70
Laud, William, Archbishop of Canter-
    bury, 1, 31, 34, 81, 87, 113, 117
Leicester, Earl of, 70
Lennox, Duke of, 97–8
Leveson, Sir Richard, 84
Lilburne, John, 34, 57
Lilly, William, 16
Lisle, Lord, 46, 70
Littleton, Sir Edward, 36
Llwyd, Morgan, 65
Lucas, Sir John, 13–14, 16
Lucy, Richard, 70
Ludlow, Edmund, 42, 53, 57, 85

Macaulay, Thomas, 94, 95, 101
Man, Mr, 15
Manchester, Earl of, 38
Manning, Dr Brian, 59, 121
Mannocke, Sir Francis, 15
Mansell, Sir Robert, 4
Marten, Henry, 42, 53
Martin, Mr, 15
Marx, Karl, 96–104, 106–7
Mason, Thomas, 68
Milton, John, 45, 56, 62
Monck, George, Duke of Albemarle, 70
Montagu, Edward, Earl of Sandwich,
    70

Mounson, Lord, 46

Nayler, James, 83
Newcastle, Earl of, 18
Nicholas, Edward, 31
Northumberland, Earl of, see Percy,
    Algernon

Okey, Colonel, 46
O'Neill, Sir Phelim, 22

Packer, William, 68
Percy, Algernon, Earl of Northumber-
    land, 38
Pickering, Sir Gilbert, 70
Poulett, Lord, 17
Powell, Vavasour, 65, 66, 74
Pride, Colonel, 46
Prynne, William, 34, 105
Pye, Robert, 31
Pym, John, 5, 10–11, 28, 30–3, 35,
    37–8

Rich, Robert, 68, 76
Richelieu, Cardinal, 25–6, 79
Rivers, Countess, 14–15
Roberts, Sir William, 70
Rogers, James Thorold, 96
Rogers, John, 66, 75–6
Rohan, Henri, duc de, 112
Rous, John, 15

St John, Oliver, 26, 31
Sandwich, Earl of, see Montagu,
    Edward
Saunders, Thomas, 68
Saye and Sele, Lord, 31, 107
Scawen, Robert, 31
Shaftesbury, Earl of, see Ashley
    Cooper, Anthony
Skippon, Philip, Major-General, 83
Southampton, Earl of, 23
Squibb, Arthur, 73–4
Stanley, James, Earl of Derby, 38
Strafford, Earl of, Thomas Wentworth,
    3, 28, 29, 31, 51, 87, 111, 113, 116,
    119–20
Strickland, Walter, 70
Sydenham, William, 70

Tawney, Professor R. H., 93, 120
Thurloe, John, 76, 85, 86

Trevor-Roper, Professor H., 71, 93–4, 102–4

Uvedale, Sir William, 29–30

Van Dyck, Sir Anthony, 49
Vane, Sir Henry, the Elder, 32
Vane, Sir Henry (Harry), the Younger, 42
Vavasour, Colonel, 29
Venner, Thomas, 76

Waller, Edmund, 33
Wallington, Nehemiah, 6, 8
Walwyn, William, 121
Warren, Dr, 15

Wentworth, Thomas, *see* Strafford, Earl of,
Whalley, Major-General, 82, 86
Whitelock, James, 25
Whitelocke, Bulstrode, 46
Widdrington, Sir Thomas, 46
Whittaker, Lawrence, 31
Wigan, John, 68
Williams, Roger, 62
Wilson, Arthur, 14–16
Windebank, Sir Francis, 31
Wolseley, Sir Charles, 70
Worcester, Earl of, 4, 5
Worsley, Charles, Major-General, 85, 86
Wyatt, Sir Thomas, 22